AuthorsDoor Edition

Elements of Style Revisited

AuthorsDoor Leadership Program
Books and Courses

(See Bibliography for Book Descriptions)

AuthorsDoor Series: ***Publisher & Her World***
The Surprisingly Simple Truth Behind Extraordinary Results

Secrets that Sell Books

Websites that Sell Books

Blog Sites that Sell Books

Social Media that Sells Books

Multimedia that Sells Books

Metadata that Sells Books

Publishing that Sells Books

AuthorsDoor Advanced Series: ***Publisher & Her World***
Adventures in Publishing and the Creation of Super Brands

Writing that Sells Books

Marketing that Sells Books

Advertising that Sells Books

Branding that Sells Books

Publicity that Sells Books

AuthorsDoor Masterclass Series: ***Publisher & Her World***
Journey Deeper into the World of Writing, Publishing, and Marketing

AuthorsDoor Leadership Program for Business Owners

Personal Branding and Influence

Time Management

Power Posting

The Author-Publisher's Playbook

AUTHORSDOOR EDITION

ELEMENTS OF STYLE REVISITED

The Writing Companion

BY

L. A. MOESZINGER

AuthorsDoor Group

an imprint of The Ridge Publishing Group

Library of Congress Control Number: 2024916249

AuthorsDoor Edition: Elements of Style Revisited /
by L. A. Moeszinger

ISBN 978-1-956905-11-3 (e-book)
ISBN 978-1-956905-12-0 (softcover)

Credits

This book makes use of *The Elements of Style*, First Edition, by William Strunk, Jr., originally privately printed in 1918 and published by Harcourt in 1920. This work is now in the public domain, and it has been consulted as a reference in the preparation of this manuscript to ensure adherence to enduring stylistic and grammatical standards.

This book was reviewed for grammatical accuracy with the assistance of ChatGPT, an Artificial Intelligence tool developed by OpenAI. We utilized ChatGPT to ensure clarity and correctness throughout the text, enhancing the reading experience while preserving the author's original voice. The integration of this advanced technology played a crucial role in maintaining the linguistic precision of each chapter.

Printed in the United States of America

This book aims to concisely present the principal requirements
of American English style.

AuthorsDoor Group
Coeur d'Alene, Idaho

AUTHORSDOOR LEADERSHIP PROGRAM CALL

Taken as a whole, the information in the AuthorsDoor Leadership Program might appear overwhelming. Accordingly, due to the sheer volume of tasks, each task is presented chronologically, book by book. That said, the series are as follows: (1) AuthorsDoor Series: *Publisher & Her World*, (2) AuthorsDoor Advanced Series: *Publisher & Her World*, and (3) AuthorsDoor Masterclass Series: *Publisher & Her World*. Each series comprises **books**, **courses**, and **workbooks**, each offering distinct teachings. The courses are FREE and can be found on our YouTube channels: Publisher & Her World at Ridge Publishing Group, AuthorsDoor Group: Publisher & Her World, and Authors Red Door #Shorts.

You can also check out our other resources:

- Follow our blog at AuthorsRedDoor.com
- Subscribe to our Newsletters at AuthorsDoor.com
- Join our AuthorsDoor Strategy Forum Facebook Group
- Connect with our Facebook Page at AuthorsDoor Group
- Become a fan on our social media channels @AuthorsDoor

Please feel free to contact me anytime at info@authorsdoor.com and drop me a note; let me know what else you might like to hear from us. After all, your journey in the AuthorsDoor Leadership Program, covering writing, publishing, and marketing, is designed to be interactive, helping you make your writing dreams come true, step by step, book by book in chronological order. I hope that our work will prove worthwhile to you. When done properly, self-publishing can be an exciting and profitable business.

L. A. Moeszinger

CONTENTS

A NOTE ON THIS BOOK

In the world of writing, the foundation of every memorable work is not just its story, but the craft behind its telling. To write is to embark on a journey, and every journey is enriched by a reliable compass. Drawing inspiration from a classic, *The Elements of Style* by William Strunk, Jr., the "AuthorsDoor In-House Style Guide" seeks to be that compass for the modern writer. The first edition of Strunk's guide was a beacon for many, shedding light on the intricacies of the English language and the art of composition. With time, while the essence of his teachings remains revered, the dynamics of language and communication continue to evolve.

This guide, while rooted in Strunk's foundational principles, is tailored to meet the contemporary needs of authors, editors, and proofreaders at AuthorsDoor. It's not just about adhering to grammatical rules but understanding the rhythm, nuance, and heartbeat of modern prose. Through this guide, we aim to bridge the time-tested wisdom of the past with the ever-evolving landscape of present-day writing. Thus, as you peruse its pages, let the "AuthorsDoor In-House Style Guide" be both a reference and a muse, guiding you to not only write but to captivate, enlighten, and inspire.

The Elements of Style: A Brief History

The Elements of Style, often referred to simply as "Strunk & White" due to its most famous edition, is a writing guide originally written by William Strunk, Jr.

Its concise nature and influential advice have made it one of the most esteemed references in American English language and style.

The Original Edition

In 1918, William Strunk, Jr., a professor of English at Cornell University, wrote the first version of this guide for his English students. His aim was to present clear and simple guidelines for accurate written communication. This original version, self-published by Strunk, was a mere 48 pages and covered topics such as Elementary Rules of Usage and Elementary Principles of Composition.

The White Connection

E. B. White, who would go on to write beloved classics like *Charlotte's Web* and *Stuart Little*, was a student of Strunk at Cornell in the 1910s. He was introduced to Strunk's manual during his college years. In 1957, White wrote an essay for *The New Yorker* magazine, reflecting on his admiration for Strunk and his writing principles. This led to Macmillan and Company commissioning White to expand and revise *The Elements of Style* for a wider audience.

The 1959 Edition and Beyond

E. B. White's revised edition was published in 1959 and, alongside Strunk's foundational rules, it incorporated his own stylistic touch with his chapter *An Approach to Style*. The 1959 edition was an instant success and went on to become a standard text for college courses and a go-to guide for writers everywhere. Since then, *The Elements of Style* has been updated and republished multiple times to stay relevant. However, Strunk's original rules and White's additions remain its core.

Legacy

Over the decades, *The Elements of Style* has become a cornerstone in the realm of American English writing. Many writers, both amateur and professional, have a copy on their desk as a quick reference. While some modern critics argue that certain rules in the book are outdated or too rigid, its influence on clarity, brevity, and precision in writing is undeniable. In essence, *The Elements of Style* stands as a testament to the enduring importance of clear and effective communication. What began as a modest attempt by Strunk to aid his students has transformed into one of the most celebrated writing guides in the English language.

INTRODUCTION

In the literary realm, few works command the same reverence and universality as William Strunk, Jr.'s *The Elements of Style*. It stands, even decades later, as a touchstone for writers, editors, proofreaders, and all who value the English language. Yet, as with all classics, there is always space for dialogue, evolution, and a melding with the contemporary.

This book, "AuthorsDoor Edition: Elements of Style Revisited—The Writing Companion," represents an ambitious endeavor by the AuthorsDoor Group to engage with this classic by enhancing its timeless teachings with modern insights. This guide is not merely a reflection on style but a dynamic conversation about it—a conversation between the past and the present, the established and the innovative.

Part 1: AuthorsDoor Group Commentary navigates the broader landscape of literary style guides. In every art form, certain guidelines or handbooks illuminate the path for creators, ensuring their work not only shines with individual brilliance but also harmonizes with the broader landscape. The realm of writing is no different; hence, the importance of style guides.

I: Industry Style Guides. What exactly is a style guide? Think of it as a trusted companion for every writer, designed to streamline choices and ensure clarity and consistency. In this section, we'll delve deeper into the essence and objectives of style guides. If you've ever wondered how in-house style guides differ from their more public counterparts, we've got you covered.

II: The AuthorsDoor In-House Style Guide. Our very own beacon for writers, the "AuthorsDoor In-House Style Guide," beckons. **Section 1: Introduction—Understanding the Pillars of Publishing**. Here, we unveil the intricate dance of publishing, showcasing the roles that ensure a manuscript's journey from thought to printed word is nothing short of magical. Subsequent sections—**Rules of Usage, Principles of Composition, Matters of Form, Words and Expressions Commonly Misused, and Words Often Misspelled**—explore the nuances of writing. We cover everything from the foundational rules of usage to the subtle art of composition. We illuminate the significance of form, dissect commonly misused words and phrases, and highlight those tricky words that often cause confusion. This guide is our tailored compass, meticulously crafted for the AuthorsDoor community—a mentor and invaluable resource all rolled into one.

Part 2: The Elements of Style by William Strunk, Jr. A guide that has served for generations as the beacon for writers navigating the tumultuous seas of English prose. But literature, like all art forms, thrives on dialogue—conversations between the old and new, the foundational and the avant-garde.

I: Introductory—with AuthorsDoor Commentary. Dive into Strunk's foundational wisdom with additional insights from AuthorsDoor. Let's embark on a journey back in time, walking alongside Strunk as he lays out his introductory principles. Along this path, AuthorsDoor enters the conversation, bringing contemporary reflections that add layers of modern context and insight. It's a conversation across time, blending tradition with innovation.

II: Elementary Rules of Usage. Strunk's guidelines serve as a quintessential roadmap for clear and concise expression. Navigate these foundational tenets, as relevant today as they were when first penned.

III: Elementary Principles of Composition. Dive into the art and science of stringing words together. With Strunk as your guide, discover the architecture of impactful writing.

IV: A Few Matters of Form. Form is often seen as the unsung hero of writing. Strunk sheds light on its nuances, underscoring its pivotal role in communication.

V: Words and Expressions Commonly Misused. Language is alive and constantly evolving. Strunk provides a lens into the common pitfalls of his time, many of which remain pertinent today.

VI: Words Often Misspelled. In this chapter, Strunk becomes the ally of every writer who has grappled with the vast and intricate landscape of English spelling.

Marrying the ageless wisdom of Strunk with the fresh insights of AuthorsDoor, this section serves as a bridge between the timeless foundations of English prose and the ever-evolving needs of today's writer.

Part 3: AuthorsDoor Editorial Standards Commentary. Here we focus on crafting, refining, and perfecting the written word. Welcome to a realm where writing transforms into an art form—a symphony of words, sentences, and paragraphs, meticulously crafted to engage, enchant, and enlighten.

VII: Style Considerations and Techniques. This section comprises just a single chapter with twenty-one points:

1. The art of subtle storytelling: Unravel the magic of saying more with less, weaving tales that linger in the mind.

2. The dance of authentic writing: Discover how genuineness sways in perfect rhythm with words to create a lasting bond with readers.

3. Plotting the path: Design the journey of your narrative to lead readers through every twist and turn.

4. Creating masterpieces with words: Just as artists wield brushes, writers craft literary masterpieces, one word at a time.

5. Sculpting your story to perfection: Delve into the art of chiseling and refining your narrative until it gleams with precision.

6. Finding the perfect writing recipe: Stir in rhythm, sprinkle in emotion, and discover the perfect blend to craft captivating prose.

7. Crafting credible narratives: Build trust with every line to ensure your tales resonate with authenticity.

8. Crafting clearer narratives without qualifiers: Master the art of precision to deliver clear, undiluted messages.

9. Perfecting your writing tone: Like tuning instruments, hone your narrative's voice to harmonize perfectly with the message.

10. Picking the timeless over trendy in spelling: Navigate the evolving world of words while holding onto the classics.

11. Trusting dialogue to tell the tale: Master the art of letting characters breathe life into your narrative.

12. Mixing the right ingredients: A pinch of this, a dash of that—crafting stories is akin to achieving culinary mastery.

13. Directing dialogue with precision: Steer conversations with purpose, guiding characters to reveal secrets, enthrall readers, and engage emotions.

14. Styling sentences for the occasion. Treat every sentence like an outfit—ensure yours always makes a statement.

15. More than just words, it's a dance: Revel in the rhythm, flow, and grace of each line and paragraph.

16. Striving for clarity in every sentence: Seek transparency to ensure each line sparkles with lucidity.

17. Serving up relevance over ego: Prioritize the reader's journey by setting aside personal biases.

18. The dos and don'ts of flavorful writing: Discover the ingredients that enrich prose and avoid those that may sour it.

19. Guiding readers through the forest of acronyms: Ensure clarity in a world brimming with shorthand and abbreviations by explicitly defining each term.

20. The risks and rewards of multilingual writing style: Dance on the edge of languages, embracing the challenges and reaping the rewards of linguistic diversity.

21. Navigating the marketplace of language: Tread the bustling bazaars of words, selecting only the choicest terms for your narrative.

As you near the end of this literary expedition within the "AuthorsDoor Edition: Elements of Style Revisited—The Writing Companion," we invite you to delve even deeper into the vast ocean of writing and style, where many hidden treasures await those eager to explore.

Our *Further Reading* section is a curated collection of titles that beckon you to expand your horizons, while the *Resources* segment unveils an arsenal of state-of-the-art editing and writing software tools, perfect for the modern scribe.

If you've stumbled upon terms that piqued your curiosity, our *Glossary* is ready to elucidate. For those yearning to trace the roots of our references, the *Bibliography* provides a detailed roadmap.

Lastly, as you've journeyed with us through these pages, perhaps you're curious about the minds behind the words. *About the Author* offers a glimpse into the life and ethos of the guiding spirit of this tome.

May this backmatter serve both as a compass and as further inspiration, guiding your continued voyage in the wondrous world of writing.

Finally, we hope the content in this book, "AuthorsDoor Edition: Elements of Style Revisited—The Writing Companion," will demystify the art of writing. Let's celebrate the art of writing, the subtleties of style, and the power of clear, concise, and captivating communication.

AUTHORSDOOR EDITION

ELEMENTS OF STYLE REVISITED

PART 1

AUTHORSDOOR GROUP COMMENTARY

"'The little book is a great book." —AuthorsDoor Group

The Elements of Style by William Strunk, Jr., is in the public domain in the United States because it was published before January 1, 1925. William Strunk, Jr. died in 1946, so this work is also in the public domain in countries and areas where the copyright term is the author's life plus seventy years or less. This work may also be in the public domain in countries and areas with longer native copyright terms that apply the rule of the shorter term to foreign works.

The Elements of Style is an American English writing style guide available in numerous editions. The original version was composed by William Strunk, Jr., in 1918 and published by Harcourt in 1920, which is the version we have included in **PART 2—The Elements of Style by William Strunk, Jr**. This edition comprises eight elementary rules of usage, ten elementary principles of composition, a few matters of form, a list of forty-nine words and expressions commonly misused, and a list of fifty-seven words often misspelled. The book was revised in 1935 by Edward A. Tenney, further enhancing Strunk's original guide.

Much later, E. B. White significantly expanded and revised the book for publication by Macmillan in 1959, adding the chapter, "An Approach to Style." This edition includes a list of twenty-one reminders on matters of prose, which has been modernized in **PART 3—AuthorsDoor Editorial Standards Commentary**. This was the first edition of the so-called Strunk & White, which

Time magazine named in 2011 as one of the one-hundred best and most influential books written in English since 1923.

In preparation for this book, "AuthorsDoor Edition: Elements of Style Revisited—The Writing Companion," and particularly for **PART 1—AuthorsDoor Group Commentary**, the following features have been used:

✓ **AuthorsDoor Group Commentary—I: Industry Style Guides**. The purpose of this overview is to help you decide which style guide is best suited for your writing, based on each guide's target audience, depth, and accessibility.

✓ **AuthorsDoor Group Commentary—II: The AuthorsDoor In-House Style Guide**. The purpose of this overview is to provide you with selected sections from our in-house style guide. These sections are tailored specifically for authors, editors, and proofreaders at AuthorsDoor, focusing on the writing, editing, and proofreading practices employed across our imprints.

In the concluding section of this book, "AuthorsDoor Edition: Elements of Style Revisited—The Writing Companion," we have included the following:

✓ **AuthorsDoor Glossary**—The *Glossary* section at the back of the book identifies terms of special interest and points to the important occurrences in context. Each word is followed by a brief definition or description.

✓ **AuthorsDoor Supplementary Material**—The supplementary material includes a section on *Further Readings* and an *AuthorsDoor Leadership Program Bibliography*.

"AuthorsDoor Edition: Elements of Style Revisited—The Writing Companion," PART I, serves as a prelude to *The Elements of Style* by William Strunk Jr. It features an introductory section on industry style guides and our own evolving in-house style guide for authors, editors, and proofreaders. By returning to the fundamental basics, writers, editors, and proofreaders can correct grammar and spelling in their works, improve their vocabulary, and learn the words they need to communicate with confidence.

CHAPTER I

INDUSTRY STYLE GUIDES

". . . a sure cure for doubt . . . As for my copy, a team of wild moochers couldn't drag it away from me." —New York World-Telegram and Sun

Those of us in the writing world talk a lot about style guides. But what is a style guide? What is its purpose, and what distinguishes an in-house style guide? Additionally, what is the most popular style guide for writers, editors, and self-publishers?

1. What Is a Style Guide?

A style guide, or manual of style, is a set of standards for the writing, formatting, and design of documents. Often referred to as a style sheet—though that term has other meanings—these standards can be applied generally or may be required for an individual publication, a particular organization, or a specific field. The implementation of a style guide ensures uniformity in style and formatting both within a document and across multiple documents. A set of standards specific to an organization is often known as "house style." Style guides are commonly used in various contexts, including academia, medicine, journalism, law, government, business, and industry.

A style guide establishes standard style requirements to improve communication by ensuring consistency both within a document and across multiple documents. As practices vary, a style guide may set out standards in areas such as punctuation, capitalization, citing sources, and formatting of numbers and dates. It also covers the appearance of tables and other elements. The guide may prescribe best practices in usage, language composition, visual composition, orthography (the conventional spelling system of a language), and typography (the style and appearance of printed matter). For academic and technical documents, it may also enforce best practices in ethics—such as authorship and research ethics—pedagogy, including exposition and clarity, and compliance with technical and regulatory standards.

Style guides are specialized for a variety of audiences, ranging from general use to more specific applications in fields such as academia, medicine, journalism, law, government, general business, and specific industries. The term "house style" refers to the individual style manual of a particular publisher or organization.

2. What Is the Purpose of a Style Guide?

Using a style guide (or style manual) provides uniformity in the style and formatting of a document. Good practice dictates that style guides be easily accessible and used by all members of a writing team.

A style guide commonly covers:

* **Spelling**—where several spellings are acceptable.
* **Punctuation**—for example, the use of the serial comma or periods in bulleted lists.
* **Word choice**—terminology, or whether a controlled language or semi-controlled language is used.
* **Writing style**—for example, restrictions on the use of contractions, past tense, or passive voice.
* **Formatting and typography**—formatting includes everything that affects the appearance of the words on the page, not just fonts, but also point size, bold and italic styling, and letter spacing. In this area, there aren't as many bright lines between correct and incorrect habits as in the previous bullet points.
* **Style sheets**—a manual detailing the house style of a particular publisher, publication, etc.

Since rules of spelling and grammar (among other things) are subject to change over time, style guides should be reviewed and updated regularly.

3. What Is an In-House Style Guide?

An in-house style guide is a customized guide that documents preferred styles that may or may not agree with your primary style guide (see next section). A house style guide outlines how an organization's internal and external documents should be written. These guides cover writing and formatting aspects such as word choice, tone, specific grammar and punctuation issues, and product name formatting. House style guides are also called "in-house style guides," "house writing guides," and "in-house content style guides."

Your house style guide should be an expression of your business writing goals, strategies, and, yes, style. Therefore, it should be customized to your needs. There's no reason to bloat your guide with information you're not actually going to use. It aims to address product names, the possessive form of the organization's name, number formatting, punctuation, formal language versus casual language, prohibited words, mandatory words, industry-specific terms, abbreviations and acronyms, formatting, and the primary style guide and dictionary for your company.

Benefits of house style guides include:

❖ **House style guides promote consistency**—If everyone in your company follows the same writing guidelines, documents are more likely to maintain consistency across departments and various publishing outlets (e.g., website, marketing materials, manuals, etc.).

❖ **House style guides save time**—Most of us tackle the same writing questions repeatedly: How do we write the possessive form of the company name? Does our organization use the serial comma? What words should be avoided in marketing copy? House style guides save you time by providing one place to look for answers.

❖ **House style guides are living documents**—There are no strict rules for creating a house style guide. Yours can be as simple or as complex as you need it to be. A one-page Word document can be just as effective as a multi-chapter book formatted in Adobe InDesign. In fact, shorter guides will almost always be the most useful (see the next chapter, AuthorsDoor In-House Style Guide).

In large organizations, the communications or publishing departments typically oversee the style guide. It may also be part of a larger brand style guide that covers related topics like logo usage and graphic design. The house style guide editor is responsible for updating and distributing the guide. Now that you know the benefits of using a house style guide, it's time to answer the question: Where do you find the information that should be included in yours?

4. The Big Five Style Guides in American English

Traditional authors, journalists, and those in academia usually follow their company or publisher's chosen style guide. But if you're an independent author, blogger, or business owner, you can decide which style guide is best for your writing. This section provides an overview of the big five style guides on American English:

❖ *The Associated Press Stylebook* (AP style).

❖ *The Chicago Manual of Style* (Chicago style).

❖ The *MLA Handbook* from the Modern Language Association of America (MLA style).

❖ The *Publication Manual of the American Psychological Association* (APA style).

❖ *The Elements of Style* (Strunk & White style).

The Associated Press Stylebook (AP style)

The Associated Press Stylebook is designed for journalists who write for Associated Press outlets; however, it has been widely adopted by journalists outside of the Associated Press, as well as organizations, news-centric bloggers, and independent authors who appreciate the *Stylebook's* straightforward approach to style and usage.

The Associated Press Stylebook is updated every three years; prior to 2020, it was updated every year. The Associated Press publishes it as a spiral-bound softcover, and Basic Books releases it as a bound softcover. It is also available through a subscription-based website.

Pros: With special sections dedicated to business, fashion, food, religion, and sports, *The Associated Press Stylebook* is an obvious choice for bloggers, authors, and organizations writing news-centric content on those topics. Additionally, the *Stylebook's* alphabetized organization makes it easy to navigate.

Cons: Because it's updated more frequently than the other guides, *The Associated Press Stylebook* challenges writers and editors to stay current. Additionally, it defers to *Webster's New World College Dictionary* rather than *Merriam-Webster's Collegiate Dictionary*, which is the preferred dictionary for the other four style guides mentioned in this chapter.

The Chicago Manual of Style (Chicago Style)

The Chicago Manual of Style is the most popular style guide in the publishing industry because it's the most comprehensive option currently available. This depth makes it versatile for a variety of content, including academic research papers, business reports, and published manuscripts.

The University of Chicago published the 17th edition of *The Chicago Manual of Style* in 2017. Subscribers to *The Chicago Manual of Style Online* have access to web-based versions of both the 16th and 17th editions. None of the editions are available as an e-book.

Pros: *The Chicago Manual of Style* is a publishing industry standard, although not all publishing houses use it. Those who choose to follow it are in good company with many heavy hitters of the writing world. More importantly, *The Chicago Manual of Style* offers more depth than the other style guides discussed here. If you have questions about punctuation, capitalization, abbreviations, or other usage issues, you're likely to find answers within this hefty digest.

Cons: It's big! Therefore, don't plan on lugging it to your writing sessions at the coffee shop unless you have a large bag and a strong back. Of course, if you need a travel-friendly option, you can subscribe to the online version. Additionally, its length and density can be overwhelming, particularly if you're searching for topics that aren't directly listed in the index.

NOTE: We recommend *The Chicago Manual of Style*. To learn more about *The Chicago Manual of Style*, you can watch our FREE course on our YouTube channel, AuthorsDoor Group. Look for the title, AuthorsDoor Series: *Publisher & Her World*: "Secrets that Sell Books," and listen to the Bonus Chapter: "In-House Content Style Guide" segment. For a transcript of this course, you can purchase the course workbook titled, "AuthorsDoor Publisher & Her World Workbook: Secrets that Sell Books" (available in print on Amazon.com).

The MLA Handbook (MLA style)

The Modern Language Association of America's *MLA Handbook* is geared toward humanities students. Although it provides some style and usage recommendations, its primary focus is on documentation and citation. It is available in both softcover and e-book formats.

The *MLA Handbook* had a companion titled *The MLA Style Manual and Guide to Scholarly Publishing*. This manual was more comprehensive than the current handbook; however, the Modern Language Association stopped publishing it in 2016, and its recommendations are no longer part of MLA style.

Pros: The *MLA Handbook* is widely used by colleges and universities across the United States, making knowledge of MLA style a significant advantage for anyone involved with academic writing in the humanities or other liberal arts. Furthermore, it's physically small and therefore travel-friendly.

Cons: Given its focus on documentation and citation over style and usage, the *MLA Handbook* may not be practical outside of academic or research settings.

The Publication Manual of the
American Psychological Association (APA style)

The *Publication Manual of the American Psychological Association* is designed for academic writing and research in the social and behavioral sciences. It is also an excellent resource for bloggers and independent authors who write about topics in these fields.

The *Publication Manual* is available in softcover, hardcover, and spiral-bound version, as well as an e-book. Additionally, the American Psychological Association offers a subscription-based web portal called *Academic Writer*, which provides tools and resources for students and researchers using APA style.

Pros: The *Publication Manual of the American Psychological Association* is easy to read and well-organized, with tables and figures that are especially helpful as quick references.

Cons: While more comprehensive than the *MLA Handbook*, the *Publication Manual of the American Psychological Association* is squarely focused on academic writing and research, making it difficult to adapt for other types of writing.

The Elements of Style (Strunk & White)

Given the importance of writing, which combines the practice of composition with the study of literature, writers should become familiar with *The Elements of Style* by William Strunk, Jr. and E. B. White. Strunk originally wrote and self-published this "little book" as a Professor of English at Cornell. His student, E. B. White, who attended Cornell in 1919 and later became a renowned author and essayist, first revised the text four decades later after bringing it back to prominence with an essay in *The New Yorker*. In 1959, a *New York Times* book reviewer lauded it as "a splendid trophy for all who are interested in reading and writing." White revised the book again in 1972 and 1979. A fourth edition was published in 2000, featuring a foreword by White's stepson, Roger Angell. For more details, see PART 3, *The Elements of Style* by E. B. White. Since 1959, the publisher reports that ten million copies have been sold.

As such, *The Elements of Style* remains the respected, time-tested guide to style, usage, and grammar—it is the indispensable reference for writers, editors, proofreaders, indexers, copywriters, designers, and publishers, informing the editorial canon with sound, definitive advice. It grew so popular, often referred to as a "writer's bible"—and our "writer's bible"—that we thought we would be remiss if we didn't include it among the Big Five style guides.

5. AuthorsDoor Recommendations

In AuthorsDoor's opinion, the combined editions of *The Elements of Style* by William Strunk, Jr. and the revised version by William Strunk, Jr. & E. B. White are the best options for their cleanliness, accuracy, brevity in the use of English, and simple explanations.

The Chicago Manual of Style is the second-best option for (1) general business writers, including copywriters, bloggers, and many technical writers; (2) fiction and non-fiction authors interested in traditional publishing; and (3) independent authors who want to maintain industry-standard styles and usage.

The Associated Press Stylebook is the obvious choice for journalists, but it may also be the best choice for freelance writers or organizations that (1) create news-centric content, or (2) want to instill journalistic sensibilities into their writing.

Lastly, the *Publication Manual of the APA* offers more flexibility for use outside of academia than the *MLA Handbook*, but neither is an ideal choice for business writers, fiction or non-fiction authors, journalists, or bloggers.

CHAPTER II

THE AUTHORSDOOR IN-HOUSE STYLE GUIDE

"Make definite assertions. Avoid tame, colorless, hesitating, non-committal language." —Rule 12, *William Strunk, Jr.*

The sections in this chapter of the "AuthorsDoor In-House Style Guide"—which provide general guidelines for authors, editors, and proofreaders—have been modeled after *The Elements of Style* by William Strunk, Jr., often referred to as the "little book." However, these sections are just a small part of a much larger brand document titled *The Ridge Publishing Group In-House Content Style Guide*. This comprehensive guide was developed in part by using *The Chicago Manual of Style* and covers the breadth of our operation. (AuthorsDoor Group is a division of The Ridge Publishing Group.) We think of the sections herein as "cheat sheets" or "a list of reminders" for authors, editors, proofreaders, and the like when writing for publication. In other words, the guidelines outlined in this chapter apply specifically to AuthorsDoor Group and the AuthorsDoor Leadership Program book titles.

NOTE: To learn more about constructing a brand In-House Content Style Guide, you can read the first book in our AuthorsDoor Series: *Publisher & Her World*: "Secrets that Sell Books: Unlocking the Power of Messaging—Captivate Readers, Influence Minds, and Skyrocket Your Business Success." This book is published by the AuthorsDoor Leadership Program, an imprint of AuthorsDoor Group, a division of The Ridge Publishing Group. Available on Amazon.com.

The "AuthorsDoor In-House Style Guide"—general guidelines for authors, editors, and proofreaders—incorporates Strunk's teachings, intended for use in American English instruction, where the practice of composition is combined with the study of literature. It aims to succinctly present the principal requirements of plain English style. Furthermore, it seeks to ease the tasks of publishers and authors by focusing on a few essentials in Rules of Usage and Principles of Composition—the most commonly violated rules and principles. The Style Sheets serve as references for correcting manuscripts. After writers have learned to write plain English adequate for everyday uses through this guidance, they should turn to the study of the masters of literature for deeper stylistic insights.

Advanced Suggested Readings

The following books are recommended for reference or further study:

- ❖ F. Howard Collins, *Author and Printer*.
- ❖ The University of Chicago Press, *The Chicago Manual of Style*.
- ❖ T. L. De Vinne, *Correct Composition*.
- ❖ Horace Hart, *Rules for Compositors and Printers*.
- ❖ George McLane Wood, *Extracts from the Style-Book of the Government Printing Office* (USGPO).
- ❖ Sir Arthur Quiller-Couch, *The Art of Writing*.
- ❖ George McLane Wood, *Suggestions to Authors*.
- ❖ John Leslie Hall, *English Usage*.
- ❖ James P. Kelly, *Workmanship in Words*.

NOTE: The information contained herein covers only a small portion of the field of English style. However, the experience of our writers and editors has shown that beyond the essentials, authors benefit most from individual instruction based on the challenges of their own work; each author-publisher has their own preferred theories, which they favor over those offered by textbooks. For your convenience, we have provided a quick reference summary of this book from the AuthorsDoor Leadership Program, titled "In-House Content Style Guide," which includes a suggested Style Guide Template. This is available as a FREE downloadable PDF for subscribers to our AuthorsDoor Leadership Program Newsletter. Access it on our website at www.authorsdoor.com under Resources.

AuthorsDoor In-House Style Guide
for Authors, Editors, and Proofreaders

Welcome to the heart of the craft! For our authors, editors, and proofreaders, these guidelines serve as essential tools to ensure clarity, coherence, and polish in your writing. Whether you're crafting a narrative, fine-tuning its structure, or preparing it for publication, these directives are vital. Together, with the tailored insights from your editors and publishers, we'll elevate each manuscript to its fullest potential. Delve into these sections; they're your treasury of writing and editing wisdom!

- ❖ **Section 1: Introduction.** Welcome to AuthorsDoor! If you are an author, editor, or proofreader with us, dive into this section. It's your roadmap to understanding the roles within English writing. Let's make a lasting first impression together!

- ❖ **Section 2: Rules of Usage.** Welcome, AuthorsDoor community! Whether you're crafting a tale, refining prose, or ensuring textual perfection, our Rules of Usage will guide you. Dive into this section and let's uphold our gold standard together!

- ❖ **Section 3: Principles of Composition.** Journey with us to Section 3, dear AuthorsDoor family! For every storyteller, editor, and proofreader, mastering the art of composition is key. Let's unravel the secrets together and elevate our craft with these guiding principles!

- ❖ **Section 4: A Few Matters of Form.** Step into Section 4, esteemed AuthorsDoor creatives! Delving into the nuances of form can elevate our work to artistry. Whether you are authoring, editing, or proofreading, let's finesse the details together and excel in our craft!

- ❖ **Section 5: Words and Expressions Commonly Misused.** Welcome to Section 5, AuthorsDoor aficionados! Words are our tools, and precision is our aim. Navigate the labyrinth of commonly misused expressions with us to ensure that every word resonates with purpose. Let's conquer language pitfalls together, united in our mission!

- ❖ **Section 6: Words Often Misspelled.** Venture into Section 6, brilliant minds of AuthorsDoor! Spelling is the silent song of written words, and we aim for perfect notes. Together, let's sidestep those pesky spelling snares and craft prose that is pitch-perfect in every way!

❖ **Section 7: Style Considerations and Techniques.** Step into the realm of Section 7, esteemed AuthorsDoor artisans! Style is the unique signature of our stories. Together, let's explore nuances, finesse our techniques, and ensure our narrative voice stands out. Dive in, and let's make every word stylistically captivating!

6. Section 1: Introduction— Understanding the Pillars of Publishing

In the vast orchestra of publishing, each role—from the author to the publisher— plays a distinct and vital note. Like musicians in perfect harmony, they come together to craft a symphony that resonates with readers. The creation of a book, often concealed behind the printed pages or digital screens, is a complex interplay of creativity, precision, and strategy. In this section, we will unravel the significance of each role, illuminating how they collectively compose the literary masterpieces we cherish. Let us take you on this journey to appreciate the symphony of collaboration that defines the world of publishing.

1. **The Author: The Heart of Creation.** The role of the author is paramount to the world of publishing. They are the originators, the dreamers, and the storytellers. An author conceives an idea, nurtures it, and then translates it onto paper. They create characters, set scenes, and build worlds, sharing unique perspectives and tales with readers. While the journey of writing can be solitary, the end goal is a shared experience with the reader.

   Key Responsibilities:

   ❖ Conceptualizing and creating original content.
   ❖ Conducting research to enhance authenticity, when necessary.
   ❖ Revising and refining work based on feedback.
   ❖ Collaborating with editors and publishers to perfect and distribute their creations.

2. **The Editor: The Refining Touch.** In the intricate dance of the written word, the editor stands as a pivotal figure, orchestrating balance and precision. Like a maestro guiding a symphony, the editor ensures each element of a manuscript comes together in seamless harmony. They serve not only as guardians of grammar and syntax but also as stewards of narrative coherence, voice, and overall vision. Often overshadowed by the spotlight on authors or

the detailed expertise of specialized editors, their role is both broad and deep, encompassing various forms of editing, from substantive to proofreading. As we dive deeper into the role of the editor, we'll uncover the myriad responsibilities they shoulder, acting as the bridge between raw narrative and polished prose, and between a writer's vision and a reader's experience.

2.1 Content Editor (or Developmental Editor). The content editor plays a pivotal role in shaping the manuscript. They dive deep into the structure, flow, and overall narrative of the content. By analyzing character development, pacing, and plot progression, they ensure the story is both engaging and coherent. Content editors work closely with authors, providing crucial feedback that challenges and inspires writers to refine and enhance their work, ensuring the final product resonates with its intended audience.

Key Responsibilities:

❖ Assessing and reshaping the manuscript's structure to ensure clarity and flow.

❖ Providing detailed feedback on plot dynamics, character development, and pacing to strengthen narrative engagement.

❖ Collaborating closely with the author to refine and enhance the overall story, aligning it with both authorial intent and reader expectations.

2.2 Copy Editor. The realm of the copy editor revolves around the intricacies of language and grammar. Their focus is on the sentence level, ensuring clarity, consistency, and correctness. They polish the manuscript, making sure each sentence flows seamlessly into the next, enhancing readability and coherence.

Key Responsibilities:

❖ Correcting grammar, punctuation, and spelling to uphold the quality of the text.

❖ Ensuring consistency in terminology, voice, and style across the manuscript.

❖ Clarifying ambiguous phrases or sentences to enhance overall readability and understanding.

3. The Proofreader: The Final Set of Eyes. Often confused with copy editors, proofreaders have a distinct role. They come in after all the editing is done, meticulously scanning the text for overlooked errors. A proofreader ensures the manuscript is free from typographical, grammatical, or punctuation mistakes and checks the layout for consistency before it goes to print or is published online.

Key Responsibilities:

* ❖ Identifying and correcting overlooked typographical errors to ensure textual accuracy.
* ❖ Checking for consistency in layout, design, and formatting across the manuscript.
* ❖ Verifying that all changes suggested by copy editors have been accurately implemented and are reflected in the final manuscript.

4. **The Publisher: Bringing Stories to Life.** The publisher oversees the journey of a manuscript from a written draft to a tangible book or digital publication. They not only decide which books get published but also guide how they are produced, marketed, and distributed. Their role combines business acumen with a love for literature, involving strategic decision-making that aligns with market trends and building strong partnerships with authors and retailers to maximize the book's reach and impact.

Key Responsibilities:

* ❖ Deciding which books to publish based on market trends and potential.
* ❖ Overseeing the design, production, marketing, and distribution of the book.
* ❖ Collaborating with authors and editors to ensure the book's success in the market.

Every individual involved in the publishing process plays a unique and crucial role. From the author who conceives and nurtures the initial idea to the publisher who presents the final product, each step is essential in ensuring that the story is told in its best possible form and reaches the hands and hearts of readers everywhere.

7. Section 2: Rules of Usage

While countless grammar guidelines exist, the fundamental ones focus on sentence structure and the categories of words such as nouns, pronouns, verbs, adjectives, adverbs, prepositions, and conjunctions. A strong grasp of reading and writing begins with understanding the core rules of English grammar. This discussion will delve deeper into sentence construction and word classes, emphasizing their critical role in grammatical principles.

1. **Form the possessive singular of nouns with 's.** Follow this rule whatever the final consonant. Thus write, *Charles's friend, Burns's poems, the witch's malice.* Exceptions are the possessives of ancient proper names in *-es* and *-is*, the possessive *Jesus'*, and such forms as *for conscience' sake, for righteousness' sake.* But such forms as *Achilles' heel, Moses' laws, Isis' temple* are commonly replaced by *the heel of Achilles, the laws of Moses, the temple of Isis.*

   The general rule for forming the possessive of a singular noun is to add an apostrophe and "s", regardless of whether the noun ends in "s" or not. For plural nouns that end in "s", the possessive is formed by adding only an apostrophe. If the plural noun does not end in "s", add both an apostrophe and "s" to form the possessive. However, pronominal possessives such as *hers, its, theirs, yours,* and *oneself* do not include an apostrophe.

   ❖ A *consonant* is any letter in the English alphabet that is not a vowel (A, E, I, O, U, and sometimes Y). Consonants are characterized by sounds produced with a closure or narrowing in the vocal tract that causes audible turbulence.

   ❖ *Noun* is a part of speech that names a person, place, thing, idea, or quality.

   ❖ The *pronominal* relates to or serves as a pronoun, referring to words or elements in speech that function as or replace pronouns.

   ❖ A *pronoun* (such as *I, me, he, she, herself, you, it, that, they, each, few, many, who, whoever, whose, someone, everybody,* etc.) is a word that takes the place of a noun. In the sentence *Jake saw Erica, and he kissed her*, the pronouns *he* and *her* take the place of *Jake* and *Erica*, respectively. Pronouns can be classified into several types, including subject (e.g., *he*), object (e.g., *him*), possessive (e.g., *his*), and reflexive (e.g., *himself*).

2. **In a series of three or more terms with a single conjunction, use a comma after each term except the last.** This comma is often referred to as the "serial comma." Thus write, *red, white, and blue*; *honest, energetic, but headstrong*; *He opened the letter, read it, and made a note of its contents.* However, in the names of business firms, the last comma is omitted, as *Brown, Shipley and Company.*

    The abbreviation *etc.* is typically preceded by a comma, even if only a single term comes before it. This practice follows the general punctuation rule for lists, ensuring clarity and consistency.

    ❖ A *conjunction* is a word that joins words, phrases, or clauses within a sentence. Conjunctions can be used as single words or in pairs. For example, *and*, *but*, and *or* are used individually, whereas *neither/nor* and *either/or* are examples of conjunction pairs.

3. **Enclose parenthetic expressions between commas.** *The best way to see a country, unless you are pressed for time, is to travel on foot.* Applying this rule can be challenging; it is often difficult to decide whether a single word, such as *however*, or a brief phrase should be considered parenthetic. If the interruption to the flow of the sentence is slight, the writer may safely omit the commas. However, regardless of whether the interruption is slight or considerable, it is crucial never to omit one comma and leave the other. Incorrect punctuation such as in *Marjorie's husband, Colonel Nelson, paid us a visit yesterday*, or *My brother, you will be pleased to hear, is now in perfect health*, should be avoided. Both examples should have commas both before and after the parenthetic expressions.

    Nonrestrictive relative clauses are, in accordance with this rule, set off by commas. For example, the sentence *The audience, which had at first been indifferent, became more and more interested*, is correctly punctuated. Similar clauses introduced by *where* and *when* are punctuated in the same manner. For instance, *In 1769, when Napoleon was born, Corsica had but recently been acquired by France*, and *Nether Stowey, where Coleridge wrote The Rime of the Ancient Mariner, is a few miles from Bridgewater.* In these sentences, the clauses introduced by *which*, *when*, and *where* are nonrestrictive; they do not limit the application of the words on which they depend but add, parenthetically, statements supplementing those in the principal clauses. Each sentence is a combination of two statements that might have been made independently.

Restrictive relative clauses are not set off by commas because they are essential to the meaning of the sentence. For example, in the sentence *The candidate who best meets these requirements will obtain the place*, the relative clause *who best meets these requirements* restricts the application of the word *candidate* to a single person. Unlike nonrestrictive clauses, this sentence cannot be split into two independent statements without losing its original meaning.

The abbreviations *etc.* is usually preceded by a comma, and except at the end of a sentence, it may be followed by one. The abbreviation *jr.* when used after a person's name, is traditionally preceded by a comma, though modern usage often omits it.

❖ *Too many commas can clutter a sentence*. If your independent clauses contain commas, consider using a semicolon before the conjunction for clearer separation. While this practice may seem outdated to some, it remains a valid option for improving readability when sentences are complex.

❖ *Do not use a comma to join two list items in a list*. Avoid using a comma before a conjunction that joins two simple items, such as in *Burger and fries*.

❖ **When listing three or more items, the use of the serial comma**—also known as the Oxford comma—varies by convention. In the United States, it is standard to use a comma before the conjunction in a series (e.g., *apples, oranges, and bananas*). However, in the United Kingdom, this final comma is typically omitted (e.g., *apples, oranges and bananas*).

4. **Place a comma before *and* or *but* when introducing an independent clause**. For example: *The early records of the city have disappeared, **and** the story of its first years can no longer be reconstructed. The situation is perilous, **but** there is still one chance of escape.* These sentences, when taken out of context, might seem to require rewriting because the second clause can

appear as an afterthought. This is often because *and* is a non-specific connective that simply indicates a relationship between the clauses without defining it. In the examples above, the relationship is one of cause and result.

To make the relationship clearer or to enhance the flow, these sentences could be rewritten with subordinate clauses or phrases: *As the early records of the city have disappeared, the story of its first years can no longer be reconstructed. Although the situation is perilous, there is still one chance of escape.* Alternatively: *Owing to the disappearance of the early records of the city, the story of its first years can no longer be reconstructed. In this perilous situation, there is still one chance of escape.*

Two-part sentences where the second part is introduced by conjunctions such as *as* (in the sense of *because*), *for, or, nor*, and *while* (meaning *and at the same time*) typically require a comma before the conjunction.

If a dependent clause or an introductory phrase that requires a comma precedes the second independent clause, no comma is needed after the conjunction. *The situation is perilous, but if we are prepared to act promptly, there is still one chance of escape.* (For two-part sentences connected by an adverb, see the next section.)

5. **Do not join independent clauses with just a comma.** If two or more clauses, grammatically complete and not joined by a conjunction, are to form a single compound sentence, the proper mark of punctuation is a semicolon. For example: *It is nearly half past five; we cannot reach town before dark.* Alternatively, it is equally correct to write these as two separate sentences, replacing the semicolons with periods. *It is nearly half past five. We cannot reach town before dark.*

If a conjunction is inserted, the proper mark is a comma (Rule 4). *It is nearly half past five,* **and** *we cannot reach town before dark.* Note that if the second clause is preceded by an adverb, such as *accordingly, besides, so, then, therefore*, or *thus*, and not by a conjunction, the semicolon is still required. *I had never been in the place before; so I had difficulty in finding my way about.*

In general, however, it is best to avoid using *so* in this manner when writing; there is a danger that the writer who uses it may rely on it too often. A simple and usually effective correction is to omit *so* and begin the first clause with *as*: *As I had never been in the place before, I had difficulty in finding my way about.* However, if the clauses are very short and similar in form, using a comma is usually permissible: *Man proposes, God disposes.*

❖ An *adverb* is a word that modifies a verb, providing additional information about how, when, where, to what extent, or under what conditions the action occurs. Adverbs can also modify adjectives, other adverbs, phrases, or even entire sentences. Most adverbs are formed by adding *-ly* to an adjective. If the adjective ends in *-y*, it usually changes to *-ily* (e.g., *happy* becomes *happily*).

❖ A *verb* is a word used to describe an action, state, or occurrence, forming the main part of the predicate of a sentence.

❖ An *adjective* describes or modifies nouns and pronouns in a sentence.

6. **Do not break sentences in two.** In other words, do not use periods where commas are appropriate. For example, the sentence *I met them on a Cunard liner several years ago. Coming home from Liverpool to New York.* is incorrect because the second part is not a complete sentence. It should be rewritten as: *I met them on a Cunard liner several years ago, coming home from Liverpool to New York.* In this corrected version, the period is replaced by a comma, and *coming* should not be capitalized.

It is permissible to make an emphatic word or expression serve the purpose of a sentence and to punctuate it accordingly. For example: *Again and again he called out. No reply.* The writer must, however, ensure that the emphasis is warranted and that the punctuation is not perceived as a mere blunder. It is important to consider the context and the audience to avoid any misunderstanding.

7. **A participial phrase at the beginning of a sentence must refer to the grammatical subject.** For example: *Walking slowly down the road, he saw a woman accompanied by two children.* The word *walking* refers to the subject of the sentence, not the woman. If the writer wishes to make it refer to the woman, the sentence must be recast: *He saw a woman, accompanied by two children, walking slowly down the road.*

Participial phrases preceded by a conjunction or by a preposition, nouns in apposition, adjectives, and adjective phrases come under the same rule if they begin the sentence. For example: *On arriving in Chicago, his friends met him at the station* is incorrect. The correct version is: *When he arrived in Chicago, his friends met him at the station.*

❖ A *participial phrase* is a phrase that looks like a verb but functions as an adjective, modifying a noun in the same sentence. These phrases can "spice up" a noun by providing additional description about what it is doing or what it looks like. Participial phrases are often used in writing that needs to convey a lot of information in a few words, such as newspaper articles or fiction books.

❖ A *preposition* is a word used to link nouns, pronouns, or phrases to other words within a sentence. Prepositions connect the people, objects, time, and locations of a sentence. They are usually short words placed directly in front of nouns.

❖ *Apposition* is a relationship between two or more words or phrases in which the units are grammatically parallel and have the same referent (e.g., *my friend Sue*; *the first United States president, George Washington*).

8. **Divide words at line-ends according to their formation and pronunciation.** If there is room at the end of a line for one or more syllables of a word but not for the whole word, divide the word. Avoid dividing a word if it results in cutting off only a single letter or only two letters of a long word. No single rule applies to all words.

8. Section 3: Principles of Composition

Every piece of writing has an underlying structural blueprint. Depending on the writer's expertise, requirements, and the unpredictabilities that arise during the writing process, this blueprint may be adhered to or deviated from. For writing to resonate, it should align with the author's thoughts, though not always in the sequence they first appear. This necessitates a strategic approach. In certain instances, an unstructured approach might be best, such as in a heartfelt love letter or an informal essay. However, for most writings, intentional planning is essential. Thus, the primary rule of crafting a piece is to visualize and stick to its intended structure.

9. **Make the paragraph the unit of composition: one paragraph to each topic.** Use paragraphs to delineate distinct topics. If you're discussing a narrow topic or providing a succinct overview, you might not need multiple

sections; a single paragraph can suffice. For instance, a concise summary, a fleeting description, an overview of a narrative, or the presentation of a singular idea is often best encapsulated within one paragraph. Once written, it's wise to review if breaking it down further enhances clarity.

Most subjects, however, benefit from subdivision into specific topics, with each taking its own paragraph. This approach helps readers navigate and comprehend the material; the start of a new paragraph indicates the onset of a new aspect or viewpoint related to the topic.

It's generally advisable to avoid standalone sentences as separate paragraphs. However, transitional sentences, which highlight the connection between parts of a discourse or debate, can be exceptions.

In dialogues, every utterance, even if it's just a word, starts a new paragraph, denoting a shift in the speaker. For a clear understanding of this, especially when dialogue intertwines with narrative, consult well-structured fiction as a guide.

10. **As a rule, each paragraph should begin with a topic sentence and end in a manner consistent with its beginning.** This structure is crucial for guiding readers, enabling them to quickly grasp the central idea introduced at the outset and maintain focus throughout. Effective paragraphs, especially in explanatory or argumentative writing, typically adhere to this framework: (1) A topic sentence placed at the beginning or near it; (2) supporting sentences that elaborate, substantiate, or expand on the initial statement; and (3) a concluding sentence that reinforces the main idea or highlights its broader implication.

It's crucial to avoid ending with irrelevant details or tangents. However, it's worth noting that short, lively narrative paragraphs might not always adhere to this structure. Instead, the separation between such paragraphs can act as a rhetorical pause, spotlighting specific aspects of the narrative.

11. **Use the active voice.** The active voice is typically more straightforward and energetic compared to the passive voice. For instance, *I shall always remember my first visit to Boston* has more impact than *My first visit to Boston will always be remembered by me.* However, this isn't a call to abandon the passive voice altogether; there are times when it is apt and necessary. Yet, using the active voice regularly often results in more dynamic

writing, applicable across various genres. Many descriptions or explanations that may initially seem dull can gain vibrancy by replacing passive constructions like *there is* or *could be heard* with active verbs. For example, *There were a great number of dead leaves lying on the ground* (passive) can be more vividly stated as *Dead leaves covered the ground* (active).

In terms of English grammar, the active voice occurs when the subject performs the action of the verb, while the passive voice occurs when the subject receives the action of the verb. Verbs in English are characterized by five attributes: (1) mood (e.g., subjunctive, which relates to hypotheticals or desires), (2) number (singular or plural), (3) person (first, second, or third), (4) tense (indicating time such as past, present, or future), and (5) voice (active or passive). Here, our focus is on voice.

12. **Put statements in positive form by affirmatively stating your ideas.** Choose precise, confident language and avoid vague, muted, or indecisive expressions. Use "not" for direct negation or contrasting ideas, rather than to obscure clarity. For example, *He usually came late* is clearer than *He was not very often on time.* Aim to frame negatives positively: say *dishonest* instead of *not honest, trifling* instead of *not important, forgot* instead of *did not remember, ignored* instead of *did not pay any attention to*, and *distrusted* instead of *did not have much confidence in.*

13. **Omit needless words.** Be succinct and remove superfluous words. Strong writing is marked by its brevity. Just as a sketch shouldn't have redundant lines or a device extraneous components, sentences and paragraphs should be free of unnecessary elements. This doesn't mean all sentences should be brief or merely present an overview, but each word should serve a purpose. Common phrases often violate this guideline. For example, *there is no doubt but that* is more effectively expressed as *doubtless.* Another phrase to watch out for is *the fact that* which can often be replaced with *though* or *although*. Additionally, phrases like *who is* or *which was* can often be omitted. Instead of *His brother, who is a member of the same firm*, simply state, *His brother, a member of the same firm.*

14. **Avoid a succession of loose sentences** composed of two coordinated clauses connected by conjunctions or relatives. While an occasional sentence of this structure might be acceptable, a continuous sequence can quickly become repetitive and dull.

Inexperienced writers often compose entire paragraphs using such sentences, frequently linking them with conjunctions like *and*, *but* or occasionally *who*, *which*, *when*, *where*, and *while* in nonrestrictive contexts. If writers recognize they have fallen into this pattern, they should restructure several sentences to eliminate the redundancy. This can be achieved by using simple sentences or those with up to three clauses, depending on what best conveys the intended meaning.

15. **Express co-ordinate ideas in similar form** to maintain uniformity. This concept, known as parallel construction, emphasizes that ideas of equal value and meaning should be presented in a matching manner. Such consistency helps readers identify and relate to the content. Consider the biblical verses like *Blessed are the poor in spirit, Blessed are they that mourn*, and so on. Each follows a similar structure, making them easily recognizable and resonant.

    Novice writers sometimes sidestep this principle, mistakenly thinking that they should continuously diversify their expression styles. While there are instances, such as when emphasizing a point, where variation might be needed, it's generally wise to adhere to parallel construction.

    If one wonders about presenting numerous similar ideas, say twenty, does this mean twenty successive sentences of identical format? Upon closer examination, these ideas likely fall into categories, allowing for parallelism within each subset. If organizing them seems daunting, presenting the ideas in a tabular form might be more effective.

16. **Keep related words together by placing them close within the sentence**. The arrangement of words primarily illustrates their interrelationship. Misplaced words can lead to confusion or ambiguity. To convey thoughts clearly, group related words and separate unrelated ones. Ideally, a sentence's subject and main verb shouldn't be separated by phrases or clauses that could be positioned at the start. For instance, instead of saying *Wordsworth, in the fifth book of The Excursion, gives a minute description of this church*, say *In the fifth book of The Excursion, Wordsworth gives a minute description of this church*. Such separations can disrupt the flow of the primary statement, though exceptions exist, such as when the interruption is a relative clause, an appositive expression, or is used in sentences crafted for suspense.

The relative pronoun should typically follow its antecedent immediately. For instance, instead of *There was a look in his eye that boded mischief*, it's clearer to write *In his eye was a look that boded mischief*. If the antecedent is a phrase, the relative pronoun should conclude the phrase, unless that creates confusion. For example, it's more apt to say *William Henry Harrison's grandson, Benjamin Harrison, who*, rather than *The grandson of William Henry Harrison, who*. However, a noun in apposition can sit between the antecedent and relative, as this doesn't typically cause ambiguity, e.g., *The Duke of York, his brother, who was regarded with hostility by the Whigs*.

❖ An ***antecedent***, when used as a *noun*, refers to a thing or event that existed before or logically precedes another. When used as an *adjective*, antecedent describes something that precedes in time or order; it means previous or pre-existing.

Modifiers should ideally sit adjacent to the words they modify. If multiple modifiers relate to one word, ensure their arrangement doesn't imply an incorrect relationship. For instance, the phrase *All members were not present* might be misinterpreted. It is clearer to say *Not all members were present*.

17. **In summaries, maintain consistent tense usage.** For dramas, always use the present tense. For poems, stories, or novels, the present tense is preferable, though the past tense can also be used. If the summary is in the present, denote prior actions with the present perfect tense; if in the past, use the past perfect tense. However, in indirect discourse or questions, a past tense remains unchanged.

Regardless of the chosen tense, stick to it consistently. Switching tenses can convey indecisiveness, similar to the importance of maintaining parallel structure (as noted in Rule 15). When presenting another person's thoughts or statements, such as in summarizing an essay or recounting a speech, refrain from frequently interjecting phrases like *he said* or *the author thinks*. Clearly indicate from the start that what follows is a summary, then proceed without redundant reminders.

Summaries are often essential in notebooks, newspapers, and literature guides. They're also beneficial exercises for primary school students to retell stories. However, when critically analyzing literature, avoid excessive summarization. While a brief introduction to the subject or initial situation might be necessary, the focus should be on a structured discussion backed by evidence rather than a mere overview. When discussing multiple works, it's generally more effective to draw overarching conclusions than to address each one chronologically.

18. **Place the emphatic words of a sentence at the end.** Position key words or phrases at the end of a sentence for emphasis. The most significant word or phrase often finds its strongest impact at the conclusion of a statement. For example, the sentence *Humanity has hardly advanced in fortitude since that time, though it has advanced in many other ways* is more effectively conveyed as *Humanity, since that time, has advanced in many other ways, but it has hardly advanced in fortitude.*

Typically, the logical predicate, or the new information introduced in a sentence, claims this position of prominence. For instance, instead of *This steel is principally used for making razors, because of its hardness*, it's clearer to say, *Because of its hardness, this steel is principally used in making razors.* The strength of a periodic sentence lies in its ability to emphasize the main point by building up to it.

The sentence's beginning is the other primary position for emphasis. Placing any element (other than the subject) at the start makes it stand out: *Deceit or treachery he could never forgive.* While a subject can be emphasized when it's at the beginning, other factors, like context, usually amplify this. For instance in *Great kings worshiped at his shrine*, "kings" is emphasized due to its inherent meaning and surrounding context. If the subject needs particular emphasis, it can be effectively highlighted by positioning it as the predicate, as in *Through the middle of the valley flowed a winding stream.* This principle of end-placement for emphasis applies to words in a sentence, sentences in a paragraph, and paragraphs in an entire piece.

❖ A **_predicate_** is the part of a sentence or clause containing a verb and stating something about the subject (e.g., *went home* in *John went home*).

9. Section 4: Matters of Form

The subsequent content does not aim to provide a comprehensive overview or exhaustive exploration of the entire subject. Instead, its primary purpose is to highlight and elucidate the core requirements regarding matters of form within the broader context. By doing so, we aim to shed light on the foundational elements that are often overlooked or misinterpreted. This focus on the basics ensures that authors, editors, and proofreaders can gain a solid understanding of the most crucial aspects. Moreover, it seeks to address and rectify the most frequent violations and misunderstandings related to form, offering clarity and guidance for those who wish to navigate this subject with precision and accuracy.

Colloquialisms and slang. When incorporating colloquial or slang expressions into your writing, use them naturally without placing them in quotation marks. Highlighting them in this manner can appear pretentious, suggesting an exclusivity between you and the reader that may seem condescending.

Colon usage. The colon is used to separate two independent clauses when the second one elucidates or exemplifies the first. Unlike the semicolon, which links two independent clauses, the colon introduces information that explains or builds upon the preceding text. After a colon, the initial word should generally be lowercase unless it begins a complete sentence or is a proper noun like "Bible." When what follows the colon is a list, begin with a lowercase letter unless standard rules of capitalization dictate otherwise.

E-book. In the widely respected 17th edition of *The Chicago Manual of Style*, the term "e-book" continues to be presented with a hyphen. While linguistic evolution often leads to the dropping of hyphens over time as terms become more familiar, this particular style manual has, at least up to this edition, retained the traditional hyphenated form.

E.g. E.g., an abbreviation derived from the Latin "exempli gratia," means "for example." When it appears mid-sentence, it should be in lowercase (e.g., in this manner). Most style guides in the U.S. advise placing a period after each letter and typically recommend including a comma following "e.g." and between each example, especially when listing multiple items.

Ellipsis points. An ellipsis, represented by three dots (…), signifies the omission of words within a quoted sentence or the exclusion of entire sentences from a quoted passage. In creative writing, it serves as a tool to imply that the speaker has drifted off or left a thought or sentence incomplete. The formatting of an ellipsis can vary: some style guides recommend no spaces between the dots, while others suggest spacing (. . .). When employing an ellipsis, each dot is usually not spaced unless specifically recommended by a style guide. For example, at AuthorsDoor, we use (. . .). If the ellipsis is juxtaposed with a quotation mark, omit the space immediately next to the quotation mark.

Email. In the 17th edition of *The Chicago Manual of Style*, the term "email" underwent a notable change. Whereas previous conventions might have included a hyphen, this edition presented "email" as a single, unhyphenated word. This adaptation reflects the evolving nature of language and how common usage can influence standardized style guidelines; especially as technological terms become more integrated into everyday language. This specific alteration underscores the fluidity of linguistic norms and the importance of style manuals in capturing and reflecting these shifts.

Exclamation marks. Exclamation marks convey strong emotions such as excitement, surprise, astonishment, or other intense feelings. However, it's essential not to overuse them to emphasize ordinary statements. Writing *It was a wonderful show!* is considered excessive. A more appropriate phrasing would be: *It was a wonderful show.* The exclamation mark should primarily be used following genuine exclamations or imperative commands. For instance, *What a wonderful show!* or *Halt!* are both apt uses of the mark.

Headings. When starting a new chapter in a manuscript, it's advisable to allocate ample space at the top of the first page. Position the chapter title or heading about a quarter way down the page, ensuring there's a blank line or an equivalent gap following the heading. For the following pages, begin the text closer to the top, but ensure it doesn't look cramped. Refrain from adding a period at the end of titles or headings. However, if the context demands it, a question mark or exclamation point can be included.

Hyphen. A small yet crucial punctuation mark, the hyphen is employed to connect two or more words when they come together to function as a singular descriptive term before a noun. This combined form helps in clarifying meaning, ensuring that the reader interprets the two words as one unified descriptor. For instance, when describing a *blue-green sea*, the hyphen indicates that the sea is a shade between blue and green, rather than distinctly blue and green. Thus, the hyphen serves to enhance clarity and precision in written communication.

Hyphen and em dash, or long hyphen. These punctuation marks serve different purposes. The hyphen (-) connects two or more words to function as a single descriptor (e.g., *well-known author*). The em dash (—), or long hyphen, introduces a significant pause or break within a sentence's structure. Em dashes can be used in pairs, similar to parentheses, to encapsulate a word, phrase, or clause—as demonstrated here—or stand alone to separate a sentence fragment from its main section. Conventionally, the em dash is used with no spaces flanking it, marking a distinct style choice. However, many newspapers diverge from this convention. Those adhering to AP (Associated Press) style, for instance, place a space both before and after the em dash, creating a visually distinct format.

Hyphen, en dash, or short hyphen. The en dash, situated in length between the brief hyphen and the longer em dash, serves a specific purpose in punctuation. Distinct in its function, the en dash is employed to represent spans or ranges, most commonly in numbers and dates. For instance, when indicating a range between dates or pages, like "1990–2000" or "pages 32–45," the en dash is the preferred choice. Its unique length and purpose provide clarity and precision in written communication, ensuring that ranges are understood clearly by the reader.

I.e. This abbreviation is derived from Latin and stands for "id est," which translates to "in other words." When it appears within a sentence, it should be presented in lowercase (i.e., as demonstrated here). A majority of U.S. style guides advise placing a period after each letter in "i.e." Typically, you should follow "i.e." with a comma, and if you're listing multiple items, separate them with commas as well.

Internet. In its early usage, the term "internet" was capitalized as it was considered a proper noun. However, as the concept became ubiquitous and deeply integrated into daily life, the trend shifted towards treating "internet" as a generic noun, leading to its common lowercase representation in recent years.

Italics in text. Italics serve as a tool to highlight specific words or phrases, acting as a spotlight in written content. They are used to ensure that particular portions of text, especially those deemed critical or surprising, stand out. By italicizing these segments, writers can guide readers to take note of essential points or elements, ensuring they don't gloss over them. Italics are also frequently used for the titles of books, films, television shows, and other works; for foreign words that have not been fully assimilated into English: and for scientific names of species, enhancing the clarity and readability of written materials.

Jr. in names. Traditionally, names were formatted with a comma before "Jr.," as in "John Smith, Jr." However, contemporary style, as recommended by The Associated Press stylebook, often omits this comma, resulting in "Martin Luther King Jr." This modern approach is predominantly adopted in private newspapers and online platforms. Nonetheless, for those drafting content for U.S. government publications or adhering to the guidelines of the United States Government Printing Office, the comma before "Jr." remains a requirement.

Margins in documents. It's advisable to maintain uniformity by keeping both the right and left margins of a document approximately equal in width. However, an exception arises when extensive annotations or edits are expected. In such cases, the left margin should be sufficiently broad to facilitate and accommodate these additional notes or changes.

Numerical representation. When presenting dates or sequential numbers, avoid spelling them out. Instead, represent them using digits or Roman numerals, depending on the context. For example, use formats like *August 9, 1918*, *Rule 3*, *Chapter XII*, or *352d infantry*. Roman numerals are typically reserved for formal or hierarchical numbering such as book chapters or historical volumes.

Parenthetical usage. When a sentence includes a parenthetical phrase or clause, it should be punctuated just as it would be without the parenthesis. The content inside the parentheses should be treated as if it were separate, omitting the ending punctuation unless it's a question mark or exclamation point. For instance, *He declares (and why wouldn't we trust his sincerity?) that he's sure of success.* If the parenthetical content is entirely separated from the surrounding sentence, the ending punctuation precedes the closing parenthesis. For example, *(A completely independent statement would be punctuated like this.)*

Quotations, double quotation marks. In American English, commas and periods are consistently placed within double quotation marks. In contrast, dashes, colons, and semicolons generally sit outside. The placement of question marks and exclamation points can vary, residing either inside or outside the quotation marks, depending on the context of the sentence. For formal citations or documentary references, a colon introduces the quote, which is then enclosed in quotation marks. If a quote is followed by an attributive phrase, such as a dialogue tag, the comma is placed within the quotation marks, as in: *"I can't attend," she said.* Although it might seem more logical for the comma to be outside from a grammatical standpoint, typographical conventions dictate its position within the quotation marks.

Quotations, single quotation marks. The standard practice in American English is to use double quotation marks consistently. However, if you're embedding a quote within another quote, single quotation marks are used. The convention varies in the broader English-speaking world, known as the Anglosphere. In many of these regions outside the United States, such as the United Kingdom, books typically utilize single quotation marks for primary quotations, while newspapers often prefer double quotation marks.

References, citations in scholarly works. In academic or research-intensive works where precise references are crucial, it's practical to abbreviate recurrent titles. Ensure that the complete versions of these titles are listed alphabetically at the document's conclusion. Ideally, references should be placed within parentheses or as footnotes, to avoid disrupting the flow of the main text. When citing, it's generally best to omit general terms like *act, scene, line, book, volume,* or *page,* unless referencing a specific section within a larger work is necessary. Proper punctuation is vital for clarity and accuracy. For example, a citation like *2 Samuel 1:17–27* effectively demonstrates how to reference specific passages succinctly.

Semicolon usage. The semicolon serves as a connector within a sentence, binding two independent clauses that share a close thematic relationship. For example, *She loves books; he prefers movies.* This sentence uses a semicolon to link two related thoughts about personal preferences.

Title formatting. In academic and literary contexts, titles of works are typically presented in italics with each major word capitalized. However, practices among editors and publishers can differ. Some may prefer italics with all major words capitalized, while others opt for regular Roman font (non-italicized), with or without quotation marks, but still capitalizing key words. When preparing a manuscript, it's conventional to use italics, often signified by underlining the title. However, this can vary if you're writing for a publication that adheres to a distinct style guide. Additionally, when forming possessive cases of titles, it is common to include initial articles like "A" or "The" unless stylistically omitted.

10. Section 5: Words and Expressions Commonly Misused

Many terms and phrases highlighted in this section aren't necessarily incorrect but often reflect a lackluster style, typically seen in inattentive writing. For example, the misuse of the term "Feature" illustrates that the optimal remedy is often not just replacing one word with another but refining vague generalities into clear, specific statements. Language usage is fluid, and no single authority conclusively dictates right or wrong usage. Writers and publishers intrigued by these interpretations, or those seeking deeper understanding, may find it beneficial to explore these nuances further. For additional insights, the following books are recommended:

❖ *Merriam-Webster's Collegiate Dictionary*, Eleventh Edition.

❖ *The American Heritage Dictionary of the English Language*, Third Edition.

❖ *Webster's Third New International Dictionary.*

❖ *The New Fowler's Modern English Usage*, Third Edition, edited by R.W. Burchfield.

❖ *Modern American Usage: A Guide* by Wilson Follett and Erik Wensberg.

❖ *The Careful Writer* by Theodore M. Bernstein.

Aforesaid. While the term "aforesaid" holds value in legal jargon, it can be cumbersome in everyday writing. Instead, opt for phrases like *previously mentioned* or *stated earlier*, which are clearer and more suited to general communication.

Aggravate vs. irritate. It's essential to distinguish between *aggravate* and *irritate*. *Aggravate* implies intensifying an existing problem or condition, while *irritate* refers to causing annoyance or vexation. Ensure you use each word in its appropriate context to communicate effectively.

All right vs. alright. Many are surprised to learn that *alright* is not an approved spelling of *all right*. While *alright* might appear in casual writing, educators and editors consistently deem it improper. When aiming for correct usage, it's advised to use the two word form: *all right*, which conveys agreement, affirmation, or approval. *OK* (with its variations *Okay* and *O.K.*) is synonymous with *all right* and can be used interchangeably in both casual and less formal writing contexts.

However, in very formal writing, *all right* is often preferred. Personal preference also plays a role; for instance, I lean towards *OK*.

Allude vs. elude. It's important to differentiate between *allude* and *elude*. You allude to a book, implying an indirect mention. On the other hand, you elude someone when you evade or escape from them. Additionally, *allude* shouldn't be mistaken for *refer*. While an allusion suggests a subtle or indirect hint, a reference indicates a direct and specific mention. For example, if you *refer* to a book, you directly mention it or cite it explicitly in your discussion.

Allusion vs. illusion. It's crucial to distinguish between *allusion* and *illusion*. *Allusion* denotes an indirect mention or hint, while *illusion* refers to a deceptive appearance or a mistaken perception of reality. For example, an author might make an *allusion* to Shakespeare's works to enhance the thematic depth of a story. Conversely, a magician creates *illusions* to trick the audience into seeing something that isn't there.

Alternate vs. alternative. It's essential to differentiate between *alternate* and *alternative*. While the terms might seem synonymous, they serve distinct roles. As an adjective, *alternate* signifies every second item in a sequence and can also mean a substitute in a series of two. As a noun, it refers to a stand-in or substitute. *Alternative*, on the other hand, typically represents one of two or more choices and suggests a choice between options, a nuance not inherently present in *alternate*. For instance, *when a flooded road posed a dilemma, they opted for the alternate route since it was the only alternative available*.

Among vs. between. It's essential to clearly distinguish between *among* and *between*. Generally, when referring to interactions or relationships involving more than two entities collectively, *among* is the appropriate choice, as in: *The money was distributed among the four players*. However, when each entity out of a group larger than two is considered distinctly or individually, *between* is the apt word: *an agreement made between the six heirs*.

And/or vs. or. This construction *and/or* often borrowed from legal jargon, can disrupt the fluidity of a sentence. It's primarily useful for those who write in a highly structured or technical manner. Essentially, *and/or* serves as a conjunction to suggest that any combination of the linked options might apply. In logical or mathematical contexts, it functions as an inclusive *or*. In everyday speech, however, *or* can have either inclusive or exclusive connotations, depending on the context. When clarity is paramount, consider using *either... or, or*, or another clearer structure to avoid potential confusion.

Anticipate vs. expect. It's crucial to differentiate between *anticipate* and *expect*. *Expect* should be used when referring to a basic presumption or forecast. For instance, *I expected him to look older* rather than *I anticipated he would look older*. Similarly, *My husband expected the market to rise* is clearer than *My husband anticipated the market upturn*. In the latter case, *anticipated* might merely suggest that the husband foresaw the upturn, or it might imply he took preemptive action in light of the forthcoming upturn, such as investing in stocks.

Anybody vs. any body. It's essential to discern the difference between *anybody* and *any body*. When referring to any unspecified person, *anybody* is the single word choice. For example, *Is there anybody who can help?* On the other hand, *any body* refers to a physical form or entity, such as a human body or a corpse, exemplified by *Did they find any body in the wreckage?* The same distinction applies to similar constructions like *everybody*, *nobody*, and *somebody*, where the single word refers to people in general, and the two-word form could refer to any group or amount of physical forms, as in *every body of water*.

Anyone vs. any one. It's important to differentiate between *anyone* and *any one*. *Anyone* is used as a single word to mean any unspecified individual, akin to *anybody*. For example, *Can anyone answer this question?* In contrast, *any one* emphasizes singularity and refers to any specific individual or item among a group. For example, *Please choose any one of these books*.

Bear vs. bare. It's crucial to distinguish between *bear* and *bare*, even though they sound alike. *Bare* primarily means "to uncover or expose," as in *He bared his feelings*. Conversely, *bear* has a multifaceted use. As a verb, it can signify "to endure," "to tolerate," or "to carry," such as in *bearing a burden*. Thus, when asking for patience, *bear with me* is the correct expression. Additionally, *bear* can refer to the large mammal or describe actions like giving birth or shouldering responsibilities, unlike *bare*, which is used for describing exposure, such as *bare skin*.

Can vs. may. It's essential to differentiate between *can* and *may*. *Can* denotes capability or ability, implying the capacity to do something. For example, *Can you lift this box?* suggests questioning someone's physical ability to lift a box. On the other hand, *may* indicates permission or likelihood. For example, *May I leave* *early today?* asks for permission, while *it may rain later* discusses the possibility of rain. Avoid using *can* in situations where *may* is more appropriate to accurately convey permission or probability.

Can't hardly vs. can hardly. This is an inadvertent double negative. The proper expressions to use are *can hardly* or *can scarcely*. For example, saying *I can hardly believe it* correctly expresses that something is difficult to believe, while *I can't hardly believe it* would incorrectly suggest that it is not difficult to believe.

Certainly vs. very. Some writers frequently deploy *certainly*, akin to how others overuse *very*, aiming to amplify their statements. Such stylistic habits, while they may pass unnoticed in spoken language, become more glaring and detrimental in written form, where conciseness and precision are highly valued. For example, the sentence *I certainly believe that is true* can be more effectively written as *I believe that is true*, which is stronger and more direct. Similarly, *I am very happy* can often be better expressed simply as *I am happy*.

Compare to vs. compare with. It's important to distinguish between *compare to* and *compare with*. *Compare to* is used when highlighting similarities between two things typically viewed as distinct or different in nature. For instance, likening life to a journey or a drama. On the other hand, *compare with* is employed when highlighting differences or similarities between items of a similar category or kind. For example, contrasting the workings of Congress with that of the British Parliament, or drawing parallels between Paris and London.

Comprise vs. constitute. It's important to differentiate between *comprise* and *constitute*. The word *comprise* means "to include" or "to consist of" all components directly, implying completeness. For instance, a zoo *comprises* mammals, reptiles, and birds, indicating that it includes these groups as a part of its whole composition. On the other hand, these animals can be said to *constitute* the zoo, meaning they make up or form the zoo's composition. Therefore, while the animals *constitute* the zoo, the zoo itself *comprises* these animals.

Consider vs. consider as. When using the verb *consider*, it's important to know when to include "as." If *consider* is used in the sense of "deeming" or "believing" something about someone or something, it should not be followed by "as." For example, you would correctly say, *I consider him thoroughly competent*. On the other hand, when *consider* means to "examine" or "discuss" various aspects or roles of a subject, using "as" is appropriate. For instance, *The lecturer discussed*

Cromwell, first considering him as a soldier and then as an administrator. These distinctions ensure the verb is used accurately according to its intended meaning.

Contact vs. other phrases. When used as a transitive verb, *contact* can sometimes feel overly formal or impersonal. Instead of saying *contact someone,* consider using more direct and engaging phrases like "reach out to them," "call them," "meet them," or "email them." These alternatives often convey a clearer intention of the action you plan to take and can add a more personal touch to your communication.

Currently vs. now. It's essential to differentiate between *currently* and *now,* as both imply the present but are used differently. Using *currently* with verbs in the present continuous tense can often be redundant since the tense already indicates ongoing action. For instance, instead of saying, *We are currently reviewing your application,* it's more direct and clear to say, *We are reviewing your application now* or *We are reviewing your application at this moment.* The latter options avoid redundancy and better emphasize the immediacy of the action.

Divided into vs. composed of. It's essential to distinguish between these two phrases. Typically, *divided into* refers to sections or parts of a whole, while *composed of* highlights the elements or materials that make up something. For instance, plays are segmented or *divided into* acts, whereas poems are *composed of* various stanzas. Similarly, when an apple is cut, it is *divided into* pieces, but inherently, an apple is *composed of* seeds, flesh, and skin.

Due to vs. other phrases. It's important to differentiate between *due to* and other causal phrases such as *because of, through,* or *owing to.* People often use *due to* in places where *because of* would be more appropriate. For example, *He lost the first game due to carelessness* isn't as accurate as *He lost the first game because of carelessness.* This is because "due to" is traditionally used only when it can follow a form of the verb *to be* and modify a noun. Thus, *due to* is appropriate in sentences like *His loss was due to carelessness* or in noun modifications such as *This invention is due to Edison* and *losses due to preventable fires.*

Effect vs. affect. It's essential to distinguish between *effect* and *affect.* When used as nouns, *effect* typically means "outcome" or "result." As a verb, *effect* implies bringing about a change or realization, such as in "to effect change." On the other hand, *affect* as a verb means "to have an impact on." Occasionally, *affect* can also be a noun in psychology, referring to an observable expression of emotion. In writing pertaining to art, fashion, or music, the term *effect* is sometimes used ambiguously to describe a certain style or impression, such as "a Southwestern effect" or "effects in pale green." Writers aiming for clarity should steer clear of such ambiguous usage.

Etc. vs. etcetera. Avoid using the abbreviation *etc.* when referring to people. The term *etcetera* is synonymous with "and the rest," "and so on," or "and so forth." It shouldn't be used when these phrases would leave ambiguity, particularly if the reader might remain uncertain about significant details. *Etc.* is most appropriate when representing the concluding items of a fully presented list or inconsequential words at the end of a quotation. It's incorrect to use *etc.* following a list that begins with qualifiers like "such as" or "for example," because these phrases already suggest that the list is not exhaustive and additional examples could be provided.

Everything vs. everyone vs. everybody. The term *everything* is always a single word and refers to all things or elements in a context. Both *everyone* and *everybody* serve as indefinite pronouns and are interchangeable, referring to all individuals within a group. On the other hand, *every one* (two separate words) emphasizes individuality within a collective or group. In essence, while *everyone* or *everybody* points to the entire group as a whole, *every one* highlights each distinct member of that group.

Fact vs. opinion. The term *fact* should be reserved for statements that can be directly verified or proven. For instance, a specific event occurring on a particular date or the melting point of lead are examples of facts. However, conclusions or judgments, such as claiming Napoleon was the most outstanding modern general or praising the delightful climate of California, are not facts in the strictest sense. Even if these statements might be widely accepted, they are more accurately described as *opinions* or assessments. While opinions can be informed by facts, they are not themselves verifiable facts and reflect personal or subjective interpretations.

Farther vs. further. These two terms are often used interchangeably, but it's beneficial to distinguish between them: *farther* is more appropriate when referring to physical distance, while *further* is suited for referencing an extension in time, degree, or abstract measures. For instance, you'd run *farther* in a race, indicating a measurable distance. Conversely, you'd explore a topic *further* in a discussion, which suggests a deeper or extended engagement. Additionally, *further* can imply a continuation, such as furthering one's education, indicating progress or advancement in abstract terms.

Get vs. have. It's important not to interchange *get* with *have* carelessly. Using the informal "have got" in place of *have* is generally less suitable for formal writing. Moreover, the usage of the past participle forms "got" and "gotten" varies by dialect. In American English, "gotten" is often the correct past participle of "get," whereas in British English, "got" is used. For instance, an American might say, *He has gotten no results*, while a British person would say, *He has got no results*. Similarly, for the phrase about returning without any acquisitions, Americans would typically say, *They returned without having gotten any*, whereas in British English, it would be *They returned without having got any*.

However vs. nevertheless. It's essential not to muddle *however* with *nevertheless* when using them to start sentences. Both can be used at the beginning of a sentence as conjunctive adverbs to introduce contrast. For example, *The roads were almost impassable. Nevertheless, we eventually reached the camp.* However, *however* can also imply "in whichever manner" or "to whatever degree" when placed at the start. For instance, *However you advise him, he's likely to follow his instincts.* Therefore, when *however* is used to mean *nevertheless*, it often fits better within the sentence for clarity, as in *The roads were almost impassable, but we eventually reached the camp*, instead of at the beginning.

Imply vs. infer. It's crucial not to interchange *imply* with *infer*. The two terms serve distinct purposes. To *imply* is to suggest or hint at something without directly stating it. On the other hand, to *infer* is to draw a conclusion based on the information presented or available. For instance, if one says, *Farming requires dedication*, they imply that it's a demanding job. If someone hears this and concludes that a farmer probably has a long working day, they are inferring from the statement made.

Inasmuch as vs. insofar as. Both *inasmuch as* and *insofar as* convey the idea of "to the extent that." While they can sometimes be used interchangeably, there are subtle differences in their usage. *Inasmuch as* often implies a reason or cause, effectively linking it to the rationale behind an action. For example, *Inasmuch as we lack sufficient data, we must delay the project launch*. On the other hand, *insofar as* emphasizes the degree or extent of something. For example, *The project will continue insofar as funding permits*, indicating that the continuation of the project depends on the availability of funds.

Interesting vs. funny. These terms, *interesting* and *funny*, often fall flat when used as introductory words. Rather than proclaiming that the forthcoming information is *interesting*, it is more effective to present it in a manner that inherently captures interest. Similarly, starting a statement with the word *funny* does not guarantee that the content will be humorous. The content itself should evoke the amusement, not the label. By allowing the material to engage or entertain on its own merits, communicators can more genuinely captivate their audience.

Kind of vs. other phrases. Avoid using the phrase *kind of* as a replacement for "rather" or "something like," except in informal contexts. It is best to reserve *kind of* for its literal meaning. For example, the phrase *Amber is a kind of fossil resin*, or *I'm not fond of that kind of attention*, demonstrates its correct use. Similarly, exercise caution with "sort of" in formal writing, where it can also detract from the precision and formality of the text.

Lay vs. lie. Avoid confusing the verbs *lay* and *lie*. *Lay* requires a direct object—something being laid down. For example, *The hen lays an egg*. On the other hand, *lie* doesn't require a direct object. For instance, *The llama lies down*. The past tense of *lie* is *lay*, as in *He lay down yesterday*, and its past participle is *lain*, used in perfect tenses like *He has lain down*. The sequence for *lie* is lie-lay-lain-lying, and for *lay* it's lay-laid-laid-laying, respectively.

Less vs. fewer. Ensure you distinguish between *less* and *fewer*. Saying *He had less men than before* is incorrect because "men" can be counted. Instead, say *He had fewer men than before*. Use *less* for quantities that can't be counted and *fewer* for items that can be counted. For instance, *less trouble* implies the trouble is not as intense, whereas *fewer troubles* means the number of troubles is smaller. Additionally, you might use *less water* when referring to a volume that cannot be individually counted.

Like vs. as. Be mindful not to confuse *like* with *as*. Use *like* when comparing nouns or pronouns to show similarity. For example, you might say, *He fights like a lion*, where *like* introduces a noun (lion) to compare with the subject (He). In contrast, *as* is used before phrases and clauses that include a verb, describing the manner of an action. For instance, instead of saying *We spent the evening like in the past*, the correct form is *We spent the evening as we did in the past*, because *as* precedes a phrase containing a verb (did). Additionally, it's incorrect to say, *Chloe smells nice, like a pretty girl should*, because *like* should not introduce clauses with verbs. The correct sentence would be, *Chloe smells nice, as a pretty girl should*, using *as* to introduce the verb (should). In professional writing, using *like* before phrases and clauses with verbs is typically considered an error.

Me vs. I. Ensure clarity in its usage. Avoid incorrectly using *I* as the object of a verb or preposition in an attempt to sound formal. Saying *Between you and I* is a mistake. The correct form is *Between you and me*. Likewise, *They came to meet my wife and I* is wrong; the accurate expression is *they came to meet my wife and me*.

Nauseous vs. nauseated. It's essential to distinguish between *nauseous* and *nauseated*. Traditionally, *nauseous* describes something that induces a feeling of nausea, whereas *nauseated* refers to the feeling of being sick or queasy. Therefore, saying *I feel nauseous* traditionally implies you believe you might induce nausea in others, while *I feel nauseated* correctly expresses that you yourself feel sick. However, in modern usage, *nauseous* is also commonly used to describe feeling nausea.

Nor vs. or. It's crucial to differentiate between *nor* and *or*. After a negative statement, some mistakenly use *nor* in place of *or*. The statement *He cannot eat nor sleep* is incorrect; it should be *He cannot eat or sleep*. However, when using *neither*, the correct conjunction to follow is *nor*, as in *He can neither eat nor sleep*. If emphasizing the negativity of both actions separately, one might say, *He cannot eat, nor can he sleep.*

Oftentimes vs. ofttimes. Both are archaic expressions, having roots deep in historical and literary contexts. While once common in classic literature and old writings, these terms have largely fallen out of modern usage. Today, the streamlined and more commonly accepted term is "often," which captures the intended frequency without the old-fashioned flourish. Using "often" helps maintain clarity and simplicity in contemporary writing and speech.

One of the most vs. other phrases. Consider avoiding the phrase *one of the most* at the start of essays or paragraphs. While not incorrect, it is overused and can make writing seem unoriginal. For example, instead of beginning with *One of the most interesting developments in modern science is . . .*, or *Switzerland is one of the most interesting countries in Europe*, try more dynamic and engaging openings. This approach enhances the freshness and vigor of your writing, making it more engaging and impactful.

One hundred and one vs. other phrases. In expressions like *one hundred and one*, the inclusion of "and" aligns with traditional British English usage, which dates back to the Old English period. This practice not only adheres to traditional writing styles but also aids in clarity and rhythmic flow, making numbers easier to read and comprehend in written form. However, it's important to note that American English often omits "and" in such numerical expressions, writing *one hundred one* instead. Understanding these differences can enhance precision and appropriateness in both international and locale-specific contexts.

Partially vs. partly. Avoid interchanging *partially* with *partly* without considering their nuanced differences. *Partially* is more appropriate when discussing degrees of a condition or state, as in, *He was partially satisfied with the outcome.* On the other hand, *partly* is apt when distinguishing a part from the whole, often in the context of physical entities. For instance, *The boat was partly in the water* is more appropriate than saying it was *partially in the water*. Use *partly* to describe distinct portions, while *partially* to describe extents or degrees.

People vs. public. Be mindful of the distinction between *people* and *public*. *People* is a general term for groups or assemblies of individuals, whereas "the people" typically refers to a collective in a political context, implying involvement in governance or civil activities. Conversely, *public* refers to the broader audience or community from which artists gain appreciation or businesses derive support. When specifying a number, it's generally more appropriate to use "persons" rather than *people*. For instance, if you start with "six persons" and five depart, you're left with one person. Using *people* in this context can be ambiguous, as *people* usually refers to a group in a less specific sense.

Please advise vs. other phrases. Please advise is a formal way to request information, commonly found in professional communication. In business settings, some perceive it as having a passive-aggressive tone, while in informal situations, it might be used humorously or sarcastically.

Respective vs. respectively. *Respective* and *respectively* are often used to clarify individual correspondence in lists or comparisons, but they can be redundant in simpler contexts. For example, *Works of fiction are listed under the names of their respective authors* can be more succinctly stated as *Works of fiction are listed under their authors' names*, as the possession clearly implies individual correspondence. While *respectively* is useful in sequences where it clarifies one-to-one correspondences, such as in *Alice, Bob, and Carol won first, second, and* *third places, respectively*, it's generally unnecessary in everyday prose where such detail is not needed. This distinction helps avoid over-complication and enhances clarity in writing.

Shall vs. will. Be careful when choosing between *shall* and *will*. In formal English, *shall* is typically used with the first person to indicate the future tense, expressing an expectation or inevitability (e.g., *I shall go to the market*), while *will* is used for the second and third persons, conveying determination or consent (e.g., *You will understand*). For instance, a distressed swimmer might exclaim, *I shall drown; no one will save me!* To suggest inevitability, whereas someone determined might declare, *I will drown; no one shall save me!* To express a deliberate choice. However, in casual conversation, these distinctions often blur, and the correct usage largely depends on context and regional variations.

So vs. and so. Be cautious when using *so* as an intensifier, such as in expressions like *so good, so warm*, or *so delightful*. Its overuse can dilute the impact of your statements. When using *so* to introduce a clause indicating a result or consequence, like in *It was raining, so we stayed indoors*, ensure it clearly connects the cause and its effect without additional emphasis. In contrast, *and so* often serves to underline the significance of the result or conclusion, adding narrative weight. For example, *We had run out of options, and so we decided to return home*. This usage not only links the cause and effect but also emphasizes the consequential nature of the action, making it a stronger, more formal choice. In summary, use *so* for straightforward causal connections and consider *and so* when you need to emphasize the inevitability or gravity of the conclusion drawn from preceding statements.

Stationary vs. stationery. It's essential to distinguish between *stationary* and *stationery*. *Stationary* means not moving or not intended to be moved. *The car remained stationary in the parking spot for hours*. *Stationery* means writing materials, such as paper, pens, and envelopes, often used in an office setting. *I need to buy some new stationery for my office, especially notepads and pens*.

Than vs. then. Avoid mixing up *than* with *then*. Use *than* when making comparisons, indicating a preference or difference, such as in *apples are sweeter than oranges*. On the other hand, *then* refers to a sequence in time or a subsequent event, like *I went for a run, then had breakfast*. Ensure you pick the right word based on the context.

Thank you in advance vs. thank you. Using *thank you in advance* or *thanking you in advance* can come across as presumptuous, as it suggests that the writer assumes the requested favor will be granted without further interaction. A more considerate approach is to simply say *thank you*. Once the request is fulfilled, a follow-up acknowledgment or expression of appreciation is appropriate. While *thanks in advance* is commonly used in informal settings, it's important to gauge the tone and relationship to determine if its use is fitting. In some contexts, making assumptions can be perceived as impolite.

That vs. which. Use *that* for essential clauses and *which* for non-essential clauses. Essential clauses, which are necessary to the meaning of the sentence, do not require commas, while non-essential clauses, which provide additional information, do. For example: *The lawn mower that is broken is in the garage* specifies a particular mower and does not use commas. Conversely, *The lawn mower, which is broken, is in the garage* adds non-essential information about the mower and is set off with commas. Remember, use commas with *which* to enclose clauses that add extra information, but not with *that*, which identifies key information crucial to the sentence's meaning.

They vs. other phrases. Often, people use *they* as a singular pronoun to refer to antecedents like "each," "everybody," or "anyone," even though these terms suggest individuality and would traditionally be paired with singular pronouns. The use of *they* in these instances serves to sidestep the cumbersome "he or she" or to remain gender-neutral. For example, one might say, *A friend of mine told me that they said so.* Traditionally, "he" was used for such antecedents unless referring to a specifically female subject. However, the use of singular *they* is increasingly accepted in modern English, reflecting evolving language norms and a growing awareness of gender identity.

Too vs. other phrases. The word *too* is often used to convey the meaning of "also" or "in addition." When using *too* in the middle of a sentence, it's customary to place a comma before it to set it off from the rest of the sentence, highlighting its additive nature. For example, *I love chocolate, too, but it's not good for my diet.* When *too* is used at the end of a sentence, a comma generally precedes it to include a pause or add emphasis, depending on the context. For instance: *I enjoy reading novels, and I like nonfiction, too.* This use of commas helps readers or listeners understand that *too* is adding information or emphasizing agreement or similarity with a previous statement.

Tortuous vs. torturous. Be careful not to mix up *tortuous* with *torturous*. *Tortuous* describes something with twists and turns, like a winding path. On the other hand, *torturous* relates to pain or suffering, reminiscent of the word "torture." While both terms have roots in the concept of "twisting," it's crucial to use them in their respective contexts to convey the correct meaning.

United Kingdom. In formal writing, spell out, do not abbreviate.

United States. In formal writing, spell out, do not abbreviate.

While vs. other phrases. Be cautious when using *while* in place of connectors like "and," "but," or "although." Some writers use *while* to vary their phrasing or due to uncertainty about the most suitable conjunction. In cases where *while* is used to mean "although" or to introduce a contrast not related to time, a semicolon might sometimes be a clearer choice. For instance, the sentence *The office and salesrooms are on the ground floor, while the rest of the building is devoted to manufacturing*, suggests a contrast in function within the same timeframe. If the timing or simultaneous contrast isn't relevant, it might be clearer to say, *The office and salesrooms are on the ground floor; the rest of the building is devoted to manufacturing*. Although *while* can sometimes substitute for "although," ensure it is used correctly to avoid confusion. Ideally, use *while* to denote concurrent events or durations.

Whom vs. who. Be vigilant when choosing between *whom* and *who*. It's common to mistakenly use *whom* in places where *who* should be used if it acts as the subject of the verb in the relative clause. Think of *who* as akin to "he/she" and *whom* as akin to "him/her." For instance, in the sentence *His brother, whom he said would send him the money*, the word *whom* might seem correct at first glance, but *who* is actually appropriate because it is the subject of "would send." Therefore, the correct formulation is: *His brother, who he said would send him the money*.

Whose vs. who's. Be cautious when distinguishing between *whose* and *who's*. *Who's* is a contraction that stands for "who is" or "who has." For example, *Who's coming to dinner?* or *Who's been calling you?* On the other hand, *whose* is a possessive pronoun, similar to "my" or "their." It is used when the owner of something is unknown or unspecified, as in *Whose book is this?* This distinction is crucial for correct grammar in writing and speech.

-wise vs. other phrases. Avoid the unchecked use of *-wise* as a makeshift suffix, such as in "taxwise" or "saltwater taffy-wise." This suffix is most effective when it indicates a manner or direction, as in "clockwise." Responsible writers should refrain from adding -*wise* to any noun without careful consideration, avoiding the temptation of this overused construction. In formal writing, using -*wise* inappropriately can appear informal or jargonistic. It is best replaced with more precise language to enhance both clarity and professionalism.

Worthwhile vs other phrases. *Worthwhile* is an adjective that signifies something that has value or merit, and it is particularly suited to describe actions or endeavors, asking whether they justify the effort or resources required. For example, asking *Is it worthwhile to make a call?* uses the term appropriately. However, using it carelessly, especially in terms of general praise or criticism, can dilute its meaning. Phrases like *His books are not worthwhile* are misused because they incorrectly apply the adjective to objects. A more accurate expression would be: *His books are not worth reading*, as this phrase correctly evaluates the worthiness of engaging with the books, rather than the books themselves possessing the attribute of *worthwhile*.

Would vs. should. Be careful not to mix up *would* and *should*. *Should* is often used to advise or suggest what is appropriate, as in *I should not have made it without his assistance*. It can also express expectation or prediction, particularly in indirect speech following a past-tense verb, e.g., *He said that we should expect a significant surprise soon*. On the other hand, *would* is typically used to describe habitual actions in the past or hypothetical scenarios, such as *He would wake up early daily*. When narrating repeated actions, *would* emphasizes the habitual nature, but for straightforward factual statements about frequency, the simple past tense can be more direct and clear, e.g., *Every year, he visited the ancestral home* rather than *Every year, he would visit the ancestral home*. When narrating, ensure clear transitions between general habits and specific instances to maintain clarity.

11. Section 6: Words Often Misspelled

In the world of fast-paced communications, spelling errors are more than just minor blunders; they can significantly impact the clarity and professionalism of your writing. This section delves into some of the most frequently misspelled words, offering insights into common mistakes and providing tips to ensure accuracy. Whether it's confusing *affect* with *effect*, or mixing up *complement* and *compliment*, mastering these tricky spellings will enhance your writing skills and boost your confidence in crafting error-free text. Join us as we explore these pitfalls and equip you with the knowledge to avoid them, ensuring your writing is polished and precise.

Here's a general list that includes common words across various settings that are often misspelled:

1. Accommodate – Remember it has double "c"s and double "m"s.

2. Definitely – Often misspelled as "definately" or "defiantly."

3. Separate – Commonly misspelled as "seperate."

4. Occurrence – Note the double "c" and double "r."

5. Necessary – It has one "c" and two "s"s.

6. Embarrass – Contains double "r" and double "s."

7. Privilege – Sometimes misspelled as "priviledge."

8. Conscience – Don't confuse it with "conscious."

9. Rhythm – Missing vowels can trip people up.

10. Maintenance – Watch out for the placement of "e" and "a."

11. Receive – Remember "i" before "e," except after "c."

12. Weird – A notable exception to the "i before e" rule.

13. Maneuver – Often misspelled due to its unusual structure.

14. Minuscule – Sometimes misspelled as "miniscule."

15. Millennium – Has double "l" and double "n."

16. Occasion – Remember it has double "c" and a single "s."

17. Accidentally – Sometimes misspelled with one "l."

18. Recommend – Has double "m."

19. Supersede – Often misspelled as "supercede."

20. Calendar – Commonly misspelled as "calender."

21. Judgment – Often misspelled with an extra "e" as "judgement."

22. Acknowledgment – Be careful not to insert an extra "e" after "g."

23. Possession – Contains double "s" twice.

24. Publicly – Often misspelled as "publically."

25. Unnecessary – It has two "n"s and two "s"s.

These words can be tricky due to silent letters, double letters, and rules that have exceptions. Knowing them can significantly improve spelling accuracy in any writing context.

PART 2

THE ELEMENTS OF STYLE
BY WILLIAM STRUNK, JR.

"This book aims to give in brief space the principal requirements of plain English style." —William Strunk, Jr.

A new Afterword by Charles Osgood was included in the fourth edition of *The Elements of Style* by William Strunk, Jr. & E. B. White, which is featured in this introductory section. It reminds readers that the advice of Strunk & White remains as valuable today as when it was first offered. This book has conveyed the principles of English style to millions of readers.

Afterword by Charles Osgood

William Strunk, Jr., and E. B. White were unique collaborators. Unlike Gilbert and Sullivan, or Woodward and Bernstein, they worked separately and decades apart.

We have no way of knowing whether Professor Strunk took particular notice of Elwyn Brooks White, a student of his at Cornell University in 1919. Neither teacher nor pupil could have realized that their names would be linked as they now are. Nor could they have imagined that thirty-eight years after they met, White would take this little gem of a textbook that Strunk had written for his students, polish it, expand it, and transform it into a classic.

E. B. White shared Strunk's sympathy for the reader. To Strunk's dos and don'ts, he added passages about the power of words and the clear expression of thoughts and feelings. To the nuts and bolts of grammar he added a rhetorical dimension.

The editors of this edition have followed in White's footsteps, once again providing fresh examples and modernizing usage where appropriate. *The Elements of Style* is still a little book, small enough and important enough to carry in your pocket, as we carry ours. It has helped us to write better. We believe it can do the same for you.

In the "AuthorsDoor Edition: Elements of Style Revisited—The Writing Companion," PART 2, *The Elements of Style* by William Strunk, Jr., the following features have been added, including short introductions at the beginning of each chapter where previously none existed.

- ✓ **I: Introductory—with AuthorsDoor Commentary**. AuthorsDoor has added some minor commentary along with brief summaries after each of Professor Strunk's recommended readings.
- ✓ **II: Elementary Rules of Usage**. Since the original book did not include an introduction for this topic; AuthorsDoor has provided a brief introduction.
- ✓ **III: Elementary Principles of Composition**.
- ✓ **IV: A Few Matters of Form**.
- ✓ **V: Words and Expressions Commonly Misused**.
- ✓ **VI: Words Often Misspelled**: A chapter often omitted in the many reiterations of the "little book," we have included herein.

The "AuthorsDoor Edition: Elements of Style Revisited—The Writing Companion," PART 2, aims to recreate Professor Strunk's original work with the utmost fidelity to his simplicity.

CHAPTER I

INTRODUCTORY—WITH AUTHORSDOOR COMMENTARY

*". . . Distinguished by brevity, clarity, and prickly good sense . . .
Mr. White, one of the great stylists himself, offers some advice
from a writer's experience of writing. His old teacher would have
been proud of him." —The New Yorker*

This book is intended for use in English courses in which the practice of composition is combined with the study of literature. It aims to give in a brief space the principal requirements of plain English style. It aims to lighten the task of instructor and student by concentrating attention (in Chapters II and III) on a few essentials: the rules of usage and principles of composition most commonly violated. The numbers of the sections may be used as references in correcting manuscripts.

The book covers only a small portion of the field of English style. However, the writer's experience suggests that beyond the essentials, students benefit most from individual instruction based on their own work. Each instructor often has a personal body of theory they prefer over the content offered by any textbook. The writer's colleagues in the Department of English at Cornell University have provided significant help in preparing his manuscript. Mr. George McLane Wood has graciously allowed the inclusion of some material from his "Suggestions to Authors" under Rule 11.

The following list of recommended readings from Professor Strunk's book, *The Elements of Style*, includes commentary from AuthorsDoor. This list is intended for reference or further study. The best way to improve writing skills is by reading, especially works from seminal figures in writing.

In Connection with Chapters II and IV:

F. Howard Collins, *Author and Printer*

F. Howard Collins (1857–1910) was a British indexer and writer, best known for his work, *Author and Printer: A Guide for Authors, Editors, Printers, Correctors of the Press, Compositors, and Typists* (1905). This guide, which includes a full list of abbreviations, was an attempt to codify the best typographical practices of its time. Published in London by Henry Frowde, 1905, it was reprinted in 1909 as *Authors' and Printers' Dictionary*. Collins also wrote on the philosophy of Herbert Spencer and on subject indexing.

Chicago University Press, *The Chicago Manual of Style*

Chicago University Press, *The Chicago Manual of Style*—Technologies may change, but the need for clear and accurate communication never goes out of style. That is why for more than one hundred years *The Chicago Manual of Style* has remained the definitive guide for anyone who works with words.

The Chicago Manual of Style, 17th Edition, Chicago The University of Chicago Press, https://press.uchicago.edu/ucp/books/book/chicago/C/bo25956703.html

T. L. De Vinne, *Correct Composition*

Theodore Low De Vinne (1828–1914), an American printer and scholarly author on typography, was considered the leading commercial printer of his day. Through his work with *Correct Composition* (The Century Company), De Vinne made significant contributions to the improvement of American printing and typography. He began his writing career at the age of thirty after becoming a partner in Horace Hart's printing office. A prolific author in the periodical printing trade press, De Vinne wrote numerous books on the history and practice of printing, including:

❖ *The Printers' Price List* (1871)—an item by item list of pricing recommendations for job and book printing based on systematic cost accounting, designed to counteract the practice of underbidding among fellow printers.

❖ *The Invention of Printing* (1876)—an investigation of the claims of Laurens Coster to be inventor of printing with movable type and awarding the honor to Gutenberg.

❖ *Historic Printing Types* (1886).

❖ *Plain Printing Types* (1900)—The Practice of Typography, vol.1.

❖ *Correct Composition* (1901)—The Practice of Typography, vol. 2, a leading style guide for compositors, proofreaders and authors.

❖ *The Treatise on Title-Pages* (1902)—The Practice of Typography, vol. 3, a revision of his earlier *Title Pages as Seen by a Printer*, published by the Grolier Club in 1901.

❖ *Modern Methods of Book Composition* (1904)—The Practice of Typography, vol. 4.

❖ *Notable Printers of Italy During the Fifteenth Century* (1910).

Theodore Low De Vinne Article, From Wikipedia, the free encyclopedia, https://en.wikipedia.org/wiki/Theodore_Low_De_Vinne

Horace Hart, *Rules for Compositors and Printers*

Horace Hart (1840–1916), *Rules for Compositors and Printers* (Oxford University Press). In printing and publishing houses, Hart is a household name. First used in 1893, specifically for compositors and readers at the University Press, Oxford, and officially published in its 15th edition in 1904, this concise book of rules has become indispensable to all professionals involved in the business of putting words into print. This includes details on alternative spellings, punctuation, capitalization, italicization, abbreviations, and many other aspects.

George McLane Wood, *Extracts from the Style-Book*

George McLane Wood (1850–1930) is noted for his work, *Extracts from the Style-Book of the Government Printing Office*, published by the United States Geological Survey. This work is specifically designed for the use of typewriter operators engaged in preparing manuscript for printing. It provides guidelines extracted from the comprehensive style manual of the Government Printing Office.

In Connection with Chapters III and V:

Sir Arthur Quiller-Couch, *The Art of Writing*

Sir Arthur Thomas Quiller-Couch (1863–1944), a Cornish writer who often published under the pseudonym "Q," was a prolific novelist known for *The Oxford Book of English Verse 1250–1900*, later extended to 1918. His literary criticism and this monumental publication have left a significant legacy. He is also celebrated for his work, *The Art of Writing*, published by Putnams, which continues to influence students and literature enthusiasts. Among those influenced by his teachings was American writer Helene Hanff, author of *84, Charing Cross Road* and its sequel, *Q's Legacy*. Additionally, Quiller-Couch's *Oxford Book of English Verse* was a favorite of John Mortimer's fictional character, Horace Rumpole.

George McLane Wood, *Suggestions to Authors*

George McLane Wood (1850–1930), in his work *Suggestions to Authors* published by the United States Geological Survey, initially provided guidelines for authors with a pamphlet released in January 1888. This pamphlet, aimed at helping authors prepare manuscripts for the Geological Survey, underwent a revision and was reprinted in 1892. Further guidance was issued in 1904 on the preparation of geologic folios and in 1906 on the preparation of reports for mining districts. This later pamphlet consolidated all valuable content from these earlier publications, along with much additional material, offering a comprehensive resource for authors.

John Lesslie Hall, *English Usage*

John Lesslie Hall (1856–1928), also known as J. Lesslie Hall, was an American literary scholar renowned for his translation of *Beowulf*. He authored *English Usage: Studies in the History and Uses of English Words and Phrases*, published by Scott, Foresman and Co. This work explores the evolution and application of various English words and phrases, providing insights into their historical and contemporary usage.

James P. Kelly, *Workmanship in Words*

James Prentice Kelly's *Workmanship in Words* (1916) addresses a concerning trend he observes in contemporary writing. He cites Thomas Hardy's lament about the "appalling increase every day in slipshod writing that would not have been tolerated for one moment a hundred years ago," highlighting the significance

Hardy, whom Henry M. Alden referred to as "the great master of English fiction," places on craftsmanship in writing.

Kelly emphasizes that the principles discussed in his book are applicable not only to public written communications but also to private ones, and to spoken words as much as to written or printed texts. He argues that "workmanship in words" encompasses style in its broadest sense, including all aspects that pertain to the expression of thoughts through words.

T. R. Lounsbury, *Standard of Usage in English*

Thomas Raynesford Lounsbury (1838–1915), an American literary historian and critic, born in Ovid, New York. He graduated from Yale College in 1859, and his academic excellence was recognized with honorary degrees from prestigious institutions such as Yale, Harvard, Lafayette, Princeton, and Aberdeen. In 1862, he enlisted in the 126th New York Volunteers and served as a first lieutenant during the Civil War.

Lounsbury's scholarly work is renowned for its sound scholarship and literary acumen, particularly evident in his studies of Chaucer, Shakespeare, and the development of the English language. His notable editorial and scholarly contributions include:

- *Chaucer's Parliament of Foules* (1877).
- *The Complete Works of Charles Dudley Warner* (1904).
- *Yale Book of American Verse* (1912).
- *A History of the English Language* (1879, 1894).
- *Life of James Fenimore Cooper* (1882).
- *Studies in Chaucer* (three volumes, 1891).
- *Shakespeare as a Dramatic Artist* (1901).
- *Shakespeare and Voltaire* (1902).
- *The Standard of Pronunciation in English* (1904).
- *The Text of Shakespeare* (1906).
- *The Standard of Usage in English* (1908).
- *English Spelling and Spelling Reform* (1909).

Lounsbury often emphasized that the best writers sometimes disregard the rules of rhetoric. However, he argued that such departures should only be attempted if the writer can bring compensating merit to the text. He advised that unless one is certain of achieving this balance, adhering to the rules is preferable. He recommended that after mastering the ability to write plain English suitable for everyday uses, one should study the masters of literature to discover deeper secrets of style.

CHAPTER II

ELEMENTARY RULES OF USAGE

"William Strunk taught Mr. White English at Cornell, and certainly he had no more gifted and proficient a pupil. It is a book to put alongside Fowler's works, and I can think of no higher praise."
—Dorothy Parker

There are hundreds of grammar rules, but the basics encompass sentence structure and parts of speech, including nouns, pronouns, verbs, adjectives, adverbs, prepositions, and conjunctions. Understanding these foundational elements provides a solid basis for reading and writing. To build a strong grasp of English, one should start by answering the question, "What are the basic English grammar rules?" Let's delve deeper into sentences and parts of speech to see how how they interconnect within the framework of grammar.

1. Form the possessive singular of nouns with 's.

Follow this rule whatever the final consonant. Thus write,

Charles's friend
Burns's poems
the witch's malice

This is the usage of the United States Government Printing Office and of the Oxford University Press.

Exceptions are the possessives of ancient proper names in *-es* and *-is*, the possessive *Jesus'*, and such forms as *for conscience' sake, for righteousness' sake*. But such forms as *Achilles' heel, Moses' laws, Isis' temple* are commonly replaced by

The heel of Achilles
the laws of Moses
the temple of Isis

The pronominal possessives *hers*, *its*, *theirs*, *yours*, and *oneself* have no apostrophe.

2. In a series of three or more terms with a single conjunction, use a comma after each term except the last.

Thus write,

red, white, and blue
honest, energetic, but headstrong
He opened the letter, read it, and made a note of its contents.

This comma is often referred to as the "serial" comma.

This is also the usage of the United States Government Printing Office and of the Oxford University Press.

In the names of business firms, the last comma is usually omitted, as

Brown, Shipley and Co.

3. Enclose parenthetic expressions between commas.

The best way to see a country, unless you are pressed for time, is to travel on foot.

This rule is difficult to apply; it is frequently hard to decide whether a single word, such as *however*, or a brief phrase, is or is not parenthetic. If the interruption to the flow of the sentence is but slight, the writer may safely omit the commas. But whether the interruption be slight or considerable, he must never omit one comma and leave the other. Such punctuation as

> Marjorie's husband, Colonel Nelson paid us a visit yesterday,

or

> My brother you will be pleased to hear, is now in perfect
> health,

is indefensible.

Nonrestrictive relative clauses are, in accordance with this rule, set off by commas.

> The audience, which had at first been indifferent, became more
> and more interested.

Similar clauses introduced by *where* and *when* are similarly punctuated.

> In 1769, when Napoleon was born, Corsica had but recently
> been acquired by France.

> Nether Stowey, where Coleridge wrote *The Rime of the
> Ancient Mariner*, is a few miles from Bridgewater.

In these sentences, the clauses introduced by *which, when,* and *where* are nonrestrictive; they do not limit the application of the words on which they depend, but add, parenthetically, statements supplementing those in the principal clauses. Each sentence is a combination of two statements which might have been made independently.

> The audience was at first indifferent. Later it became more
> and more interested.

> Napoleon was born in 1769. At that time Corsica had but
> recently been acquired by France.

> Coleridge wrote *The Rime of the Ancient Mariner* at Nether
> Stowey. Nether Stowey is only a few miles from
> Bridgewater.

Restrictive relative clauses are not set off by commas.

> The candidate who best meets these requirements will obtain
> the place.

In this sentence the relative clause restricts the application of the word *candidate* to a single person. Unlike those above, the sentence cannot be split into two independent statements.

The abbreviations *etc.* and *jr.* are always preceded by a comma, and except at the end of a sentence, followed by one.

Similar in principle to the enclosing of parenthetic expressions between commas is the setting off by commas of phrase or dependent clauses preceding or following the main clause of a sentence. The sentences quoted in this section and under Rule 4, 5, 6, 7, 16, and 18 should afford sufficient guidance.

If a parenthetic expression is preceded by a conjunction, place the first comma before the conjunction, not after it.

> He saw us coming, and unaware that we had learned of his
> treachery, greeted us with a smile.

4. Place a comma before *and* or *but* introducing an independent clause.

> The early records of the city have disappeared, and the story
> of its first years can no longer be reconstructed.

> The situation is perilous, but there is still one chance of
> escape.

Sentences of this type, isolated from their context, may seem to be in need of rewriting. As they make complete sense when the comma is reached, the second clause has the appearance of an afterthought. Further, *and,* is the least specific of connectives. Used between independent clauses, it indicates only that a relation exists between them without defining that relation. In the example above, the relation is that of cause and result. The two sentences might be rewritten:

> As the early records of the city have disappeared, the story of its first years can no longer be reconstructed.

> Although the situation is perilous, there is still one chance of escape.

Or the subordinate clauses might be replaced by phrases:

> Owing to the disappearance of the early records of the city, the story of its first years can no longer be reconstructed.

> In this perilous situation, there is still one chance of escape.

But a writer may err by making his sentences too uniformly compact and periodic, and an occasional loose sentence prevents the style from becoming too formal and gives the reader a certain relief. Consequently, loose sentences of the type first quoted are common in easy, unstudied writing. But a writer should be careful not to construct too many of his sentences after this pattern (see Rule 14).

Two-part sentences of which the second member is introduced by *as* (in the sense of *because*), *for, or, nor,* and *while* (in the sense of and *at the same time*) likewise require a comma before the conjunction.

If a dependent clause, or an introductory phrase requiring to be set off by a comma, precedes the second independent clause, no comma is needed after the conjunction.

> The situation is perilous, but if we are prepared to act promptly, there is still one chance of escape.

For two-part sentences connected by an adverb, see the next section.

5. Do not join independent clauses by a comma.

If two or more clauses, grammatically complete and not joined by a conjunction, are to form a single compound sentence, the proper mark of punctuation is a semicolon.

Stevenson's romances are entertaining; they are full of exciting adventures.
It is nearly half past five; we cannot reach town before dark.

It is of course equally correct to write these as two sentences each, replacing the semicolons by periods.

Stevenson's romances are entertaining. They are full of exciting adventures.
It is nearly half past five. We cannot reach town before dark.

If a conjunction is inserted, the proper mark is a comma (Rule 4).

Stevenson's romances are entertaining, for they are full of exciting adventures.
It is nearly half past five, and we cannot reach town before dark.

Note that if the second clause is preceded by an adverb, such as *accordingly*, *besides*, *so*, *then*, *therefore*, or *thus*, and not by a conjunction, the semicolon is still required.

I had never been in the place before; so I had difficulty in finding my way about.

In general, however, it is best, in writing, to avoid using *so* in this manner; there is danger that the writer who uses it at all may use it too often. A simple correction, usually serviceable, is to omit the word *so*, and begin the first clause with *as*:

> As I had never been in the place before, I had difficulty in finding my way about.

If the clauses are very short, and are alike in form, a comma is usually permissible:

> Man proposes, God disposes.

> The gate swung apart, the bridge fell, the portcullis was drawn up.

6. Do not break sentences in two.

In other words, do not use periods for commas.

> I met them on a Cunard liner several years ago. Coming home from Liverpool to New York.

> He was an interesting talker. A man who had traveled all over the world, and lived in half a dozen countries.

In both these examples, the first period should be replaced by a comma, and the following word begun with a small letter.

It is permissible to make an emphatic word or expression serve the purpose of a sentence and to punctuate it accordingly:

> Again and again he called out. No reply.

The writer must, however, be certain that the emphasis is warranted, and that he will not be suspected of a mere blunder in punctuation.

Rules 3, 4, 5, and 6 cover the most important principles in the punctuation of ordinary sentences; they should be so thoroughly mastered that their application becomes second nature.

7. A participial phrase at the beginning of a sentence must refer to the grammatical subject.

> Walking slowly down the road, he saw a woman accompanied by two children.

The word *walking* refers to the subject of the sentence, not to the woman. If the writer wishes to make it refer to the woman, he must recast the sentence:

> He saw a woman, accompanied by two children, walking slowly down the road.

Participial phrases preceded by a conjunction or by a preposition, nouns in apposition, adjectives, and adjective phrases come under the same rule if they begin the sentence. The examples in the left-hand column, below, are in correct; they should be rewritten as shown in the right-hand column.

On arriving in Chicago, his friends met him at the station.	When he arrived (or, On his arrival) in Chicago, his friends met him at the station.
A soldier of proved valor, they entrusted him with the defense of the city.	A soldier of proved valor, he was entrusted with the defense of the city.
Young and inexperienced, the task seemed easy to me.	Young and inexperienced, I thought the task easy.
Without a friend to counsel him, the proved irresistible.	Without a friend to counsel him, temptation irresistible.

Sentences violating this rule are often ludicrous:

> Being in a dilapidated condition, I was able to buy the house very cheap.

8. Divide words at line-ends, in accordance with their formation and pronunciation.

If there is room at the end of a line for one or more syllables of a word, but not for the whole word, divide the word, unless this involves cutting off only a single letter, or cutting off only two letters of a long word. No hard and fast rule for all words can be laid down. The principles most frequently applicable are:

A. Divide the word according to its formation:

> know-ledge (not knowl-edge); Shake-speare (not Shakes-peare); de-scribe (not des-cribe); atmo-sphere (not atmos-phere);

B. Divide "on the vowel":

> edi-ble (not ed-ible); propo-sition; ordi-nary; espe-cial; reli-gious; oppo-nents; regu-lar; classi-fi-ca-tion (three divisions possible); deco-rative; presi-dent;

C. Divide between double letters, unless they come at the end of the simple form of the word:

> Apen-nines; Cincin-nati; refer-ring; but tell-ing.

The treatment of consonants in combination is best shown from examples:

> for-tune; pic-ture; presump-tuous; illus-tration; sub-stan-tial (either division); indus-try; instruc-tion; sug-ges-tion; incen-diary.

The student will do well to examine the syllable-division in a number of pages of any carefully printed book.

CHAPTER III

ELEMENTARY PRINCIPLES OF COMPOSITION

". . . Should be the daily companion of anyone who writes for a living and, for that matter, anyone who writes at all."
—Greensboro (N.C.) Daily News

A basic structural design underlies every kind of writing. Writers partly follow this design and partly deviate from it based on their skill, needs, and the unforeseen events that occur during the act of composition. Effective writing must closely follow the thoughts of the writer, though not necessarily in the order those thoughts originally occur. This necessitates a scheme of procedure. In some instances, the best design is no design at all, such as in a love letter, which is merely an outpouring, or a casual essay, which is a ramble. However, in most cases, planning must be a deliberate prelude to writing. Therefore, the first principle of composition is to foresee or determine the shape of what is to come and pursue that shape.

9. Make the paragraph the unit of composition: one paragraph to each topic.

If the subject on which you are writing is of slight extent, or if you intend to treat it very briefly, there may be no need of subdividing it into topics. Thus, a brief description, a brief summary of a literary work, a brief account of a single incident, a narrative merely outlining an action, the setting forth of a single idea, any one of these is best written in a single paragraph. After the paragraph has been written, it should be examined to see whether subdivision will improve it.

Ordinarily, however, a subject requires subdivision into topics, each of which should be made the subject of a paragraph. The object of treating each topic in a paragraph by itself is, of course, to aid the reader. The beginning of each paragraph is a signal to him that a new step in the development of the subject has been reached.

The extent of subdivision will vary with the length of the composition. For example, a short notice of a book or poem might consist of a single paragraph. One slightly longer might consist of two paragraphs:

A. Account of the work.
B. Critical discussion.

A report on a poem, written for a class in literature, might consist of seven paragraphs:

A. Facts of composition and publication.
B. Kind of poem; metrical form.
C. Subject.
D. Treatment of subject.
E. For what chiefly remarkable.
F. Wherein characteristic of the writer.
G. Relationship to other works.

The content of paragraphs C and D would vary with the poem. Usually, paragraph C would indicate the actual or imagined circumstances of the poem (the situation), if these call for explanation, and would then state the subject and outline its development. If the poem is narrative in the third person throughout, paragraph C need contain no more than a concise summary of the action. Paragraph D would indicate the leading ideas and show how they are made prominent, or would indicate what points in the narrative are chiefly emphasized.

A novel might be discussed under the heads:

A. Setting.
B. Plot.
C. Characters.
D. Purpose.

A historical event might be discussed under the heads:

A. What led up to the event.
B. Account of the event.
C. What the event led up to.

In treating either of these last two subjects, the writer would probably find it necessary to subdivide one or more of the topics here given.

As a rule, single sentences should not be written or printed as paragraphs. An exception may be made of sentences of transition, indicating the relation between the parts of an exposition or argument.

In dialogue, each speech, even if only a single word, is a paragraph by itself; that is, a new paragraph begins with each change of speaker. The application of this rule, when dialogue and narrative are combined, is best learned from examples in well-printed works of fiction.

10. As a rule, begin each paragraph with a topic sentence; end it in conformity with the beginning.

Again, the object is to aid the reader. The practice here recommended enables him to discover the purpose of each paragraph as he begins to read it, and to retain the purpose in mind as he ends it. For this reason, the most generally useful kind of paragraph, particularly in exposition and argument, is that in which

A. the topic sentence comes at or near the beginning;
B. the succeeding sentences explain or establish or develop the statement made in the topic sentence; and
C. the final sentence either emphasizes the thought of the topic sentence or states some important consequence.

Ending with a digression, or with an unimportant detail, is particularly to be avoided.

If the paragraph forms part of a larger composition, its relation to what precedes, or its function as a part of the whole, may need to be expressed. This can sometimes be done by a mere word or phrase (*again*; *therefore*; *for the same reason*) in the topic sentence by one or more sentences of introduction or transition. If more than one such sentence is required, it is generally better to set apart the transitional sentences as a separate paragraph.

According to the writer's purpose, he may, as indicated above, relate the body of the paragraph to the topic sentence in one or more of several different ways. He may make the meaning of the topic sentence clearer by restating it in other forms, by defining its terms, by denying the converse, by giving illustrations or specific instances; he may establish it by proofs; or he may develop it by showing its implications and consequences. In a long paragraph, he may carry out several of these processes.

1 Now, to be properly enjoyed, a walking tour should be gone upon alone.	1 Topic sentence.
2 If you go in a company, or even in pairs, it is no longer a walking tour in anything but name; it is something else and more in the nature of a picnic.	2 The meaning made clearer by denial of the contrary.
3 A walking tour should be gone upon alone, because freedom is of the essence; because you should be able to stop and go on, and follow this way or that, as the freak takes you; and because you must have your own pace, and neither trot alongside a champion walker, nor mince in time with a girl.	3 The topic sentence repeated, in abridged form, and supported by three reasons; the meaning of the third ("you must have your own pace") made clearer by denying the converse.
4 And you must be open to all impressions and let your thoughts take color from what you see.	4 A fourth reason, stated in two forms.
5 You should be as a pipe for any wind to play upon.	5 The same reason, stated in still another form.
6 "I cannot see the wit," says Hazlitt, "of walking and talking at the same time.	6 The same reason as stated by Hazlitt.

7 When I am in the country, I wish to vegetate like the country," which is the gist of all that can be said upon the matter.	7 The same reason as stated by Hazlitt.
8 There should be no cackle of voices at your elbow, to jar on the meditative silence of the morning.	8 Repetition, in paraphrase, of the quotation from Hazlitt.
9 And so long as a man is reasoning he cannot surrender himself to that fine intoxication that comes of much motion in the open air, that begins in a sort of dazzle and sluggishness of the brain, and ends in a peace that passes comprehension. 　　—Stevenson, *Walking Tours.*	9 Final statement of the fourth reason, in language amplified and heightened to form a strong conclusion.

Another example:

1 It was chiefly in the eighteenth century that a very different conception of history grew up.	1 Topic sentence.
2 Historians then came to believe that their task was not so much to paint a picture as to solve a problem; to explain or illustrate the successive phases of national growth, prosperity, and adversity.	2 The meaning of the topic sentence made clearer; the new conception of history defined.
3 The history of morals, of industry, of intellect, and of art; the changes that take place in manners or beliefs; the dominant ideas that prevailed in successive periods; the rise, fall, and modification of political constitutions; in a word,	3 The definition expanded.

all the conditions of national well-being became the subjects of their work.	
4 They sought rather to write a history of peoples than a history of kings.	4 The definition explained by contrast.
5 They looked especially in history for the chain of causes and effects.	5 The definition supplemented: another element in the new conception of history.
6 They undertook to study in the past the physiology of nations, and hoped by applying the experimental method on a large scale to deduce some lessons of real value about the conditions on which the welfare of society mainly depend. —Lecky, *The Political Value of History.*	6 Conclusion: an important consequence of the new conception of history.

In narration and description the paragraph sometimes begins with a concise, comprehensive statement serving to hold together the details that follow.

The breeze served us admirably.
The campaign opened with a series of reverses.
The next ten or twelve pages were filled with a curious set of entries.

But this device, if too often used, would become a mannerism. More commonly the opening sentence simply indicates by its subject with what the paragraph is to be principally concerned.

At length I thought I might return towards the stockade.

> He picked up the heavy lamp from the table and began to explore.

> Another flight of steps, and they emerged on the roof.

The brief paragraphs of animated narrative, however, are often without even this resemblance of a topic sentence. The break between them serves the purpose of a rhetorical pause, throwing into prominence some detail of the action.

11. Use the active voice.

The active voice is usually more direct and vigorous than the passive:

> I shall always remember my first visit to Boston.

This is much better than

> My first visit to Boston will always be remembered by me.

The latter sentence is less direct, less bold, and less concise. If the writer tries to make it more concise by omitting "by me,"

> My first visit to Boston will always be remembered,

it becomes indefinite: is it the writer, or some person undisclosed, or the world at large, that will always remember this visit?

This rule does not, of course, mean that the writer should entirely discard the passive voice, which is frequently convenient and sometimes necessary.

> The dramatists of the Restoration are little esteemed today.

> Modern readers have little esteem for the dramatists of the Restoration.

The first would be the right form in a paragraph on the dramatists of the Restoration; the second, in a paragraph on the tastes of modern readers. The need of making a particular word the subject of the sentence will often, as in these examples, determine which voice is to be used.

The habitual use of the active voice, however, makes for forcible writing. This is true not only in narrative principally concerned with action, but in writing of any kind. Many a tame sentence of description or exposition can be made lively and emphatic by substituting a transitive in the active voice for some such perfunctory expression as *there is* or *could be heard.*

There were a great number of dead leaves lying on the ground.	Dead leaves covered the ground.
The sound of the falls could still be heard.	The sound of the falls still reached our ears.
The reason that he left college was that his health became impaired.	Failing health compelled him to leave college.
It was not long before he was very sorry that he had said what he had.	He soon repented his words.

As a rule, avoid making one passive depend directly upon another.

Gold was not allowed to be exported.	It was forbidden to export gold (The export of gold was prohibited).
He has been proved to have been seen entering the building.	It has been proved that he was seen to enter the building.

In both the examples above, before correction, the word properly related to the second passive is made the subject of the first.

A common fault is to use as the subject of a passive construction a noun which expresses the entire action, leaving to the verb no function beyond that of completing the sentence.

A survey of this region was made in 1900.	The region was surveyed in 1900.
Mobilization of the army was rapidly carried out.	The army was rapidly mobilized.

Confirmation of these reports cannot be obtained.	These reports cannot be confirmed.

Compare the sentence, "The export of gold was prohibited," in which the predicate "was prohibited" expresses something not implied in "export."

12. Put statements in positive form.

Make definite assertions. Avoid tame, colorless, hesitating, non-committal language. Use the word *not* as a means of denial or in antithesis, never as a means of evasion.

He was not very often on time.	He usually came late.
He did not think that studying Latin was much use.	He thought the study of Latin useless.
The Taming of the Shrew is rather weak in spots. Shakespeare does not portray Katharine as a very admirable character, nor does Bianca remain long in memory as an important character in Shakespeare's works.	The women in *The Taming of the Shrew* are unattractive. Katharine is disagreeable, Bianca insignificant.

The last example, before correction, is indefinite as well as negative. The corrected version, consequently, is simply a guess at the writer's intention.

All three examples show the weakness inherent in the word *not*. Consciously or unconsciously, the reader is dissatisfied with being told only what is not; he wishes to be told what is. Hence, as a rule, it is better to express a negative in positive form.

not honest	dishonest
not important	trifling
did not remember	forgot
did not pay any attention to	ignored

| did not have much confidence in | distrusted |

The antithesis of negative and positive is strong:

| Not charity, but simple justice. |
| Not that I loved Caesar less, but Rome the more. |

Negative words other than *not* are usually strong.

| The sun never sets upon the British flag. |

13. Omit needless words.

Vigorous writing is concise. A sentence should contain no unnecessary words, a paragraph no unnecessary sentences, for the same reason that a drawing should have no unnecessary lines and a machine no unnecessary parts. This requires not that the writer make all his sentences short, or that he avoid all detail and treat his subjects only in outline, but that every word tell.

Many expressions in common use violate this principle:

the question as to whether	whether (the question whether)
there is no doubt but that	no doubt (doubtless)
used for fuel purposes	used for fuel
he is a man who	he
in a hasty manner	hastily
this is a subject that	this subject
His story is a strange one.	His story is strange.

In especially the expression *the fact that* should be revised out of every sentence in which it occurs.

| owing to the fact that | since (because) |

in spite of the fact that	though (although)
call your attention to the fact that	remind you (notify you)
I was unaware of the fact that	I was unaware that (did not know)
the fact that he had not succeeded	his failure
the fact that I had arrived	my arrival

See also under the words *case, character, nature, system* in Chapter V.

Who is, which was, and the like are often superfluous.

His brother, who is a member of the same firm	His brother, a member of the same firm
Trafalgar, which was Nelson's last battle	Trafalgar, Nelson's last battle

As positive statement is more concise than negative, and the active voice more concise than the passive, many of the examples given under Rules 11 and 12 illustrate this rule as well.

A common violation of conciseness is the presentation of a single complex idea, step by step, in a series of sentences which might to advantage be combined into one.

Macbeth was very ambitious. This led him to wish to become king of Scotland. The witches told him that this wish of his would come true. The king of Scotland at this time was Duncan. Encouraged by his wife, Macbeth murdered Duncan. He was thus enabled to succeed Duncan as king. (51 words.)	Encouraged by his wife, Macbeth achieved his ambition and realized the prediction of the witches by murdering Duncan and becoming king of Scotland in his place. (26 words.)

14. Avoid a succession of loose sentences.

This rule refers especially to loose sentences of a particular type: those consisting of two co-ordinate clauses, the second introduced by a conjunction or relative. Although single sentences of this type may be unexceptionable (see under Rule 4), a series soon becomes monotonous and tedious.

An unskillful writer will sometimes construct a whole paragraph of sentences of this kind, using as connectives *and*, *but*, and less frequently, *who*, *which*, *when*, *where*, and *while*, these last in nonrestrictive senses (see under Rule 3).

> The third concert of the subscription series was given last evening, and a large audience was in attendance. Mr. Edward Appleton was the soloist, and the Boston Symphony Orchestra furnished the instrumental music. The former showed himself to be an artist of the first rank, while the latter proved itself fully deserving of its high reputation. The interest aroused by the series has been very gratifying to the Committee, and it is planned to give a similar series annually hereafter. The fourth concert will be given on Tuesday, May 10, when an equally attractive program will be presented.

Apart from its triteness and emptiness, the paragraph above is bad because of the structure of its sentences, with their mechanical symmetry and sing-song. Contrast with them the sentences in the paragraphs quoted under Rule 10, or in any piece of good English prose, as the preface (Before the Curtain) to *Vanity Fair*.

If the writer finds that he has written a series of sentences of the type described, he should recast enough of them to remove the monotony, replacing them by simple sentences, by sentences of two clauses joined by a semicolon, by periodic sentences of two clauses, by sentences (loose or periodic), of three clauses—whichever best represent the real relations of the thought.

15. Express co-ordinate ideas in similar form.

This principle, that of parallel construction, requires that expressions of similar content and function should be outwardly similar. The likeness of form enables the reader to recognize more readily the likeness of content and function. Familiar instances from the Bible are the Ten Commandments, the Beatitudes, and the petitions of the Lord's Prayer.

For example, the Beatitudes are familiar instances of the parallel construction:

Blessed are the poor in spirit: for theirs is the kingdom of heaven.
Blessed are they that mourn: for they shall be comforted.
Blessed are the meek: for they shall inherit the earth.
Blessed are they which do hunger and thirst after righteousness: for they shall be filled.

The unskillful writer often violates this principle, from a mistaken belief that he should constantly vary the form of his expressions. It is true that in repeating a statement in order to emphasize it he may have need to vary its form. For illustration, see the paragraph from Stevenson quoted under Rule 10. But apart from this, he should follow the principle of parallel construction.

Formerly, science was taught by the textbook method, while now the laboratory method is employed.	Formerly, science was taught by the textbook method; now it is taught by the laboratory method.

The left-hand version gives the impression that the writer is undecided or timid; he seems unable or afraid to choose one form of expression and hold to it. The right-hand version shows that the writer has at least made his choice and abided by it.

By this principle, an article or a preposition applying to all the members of a series must either be used only before the first term or else be repeated before each term.

The French, the Italians, Spanish, and Portuguese	The French, the Italians, the Spanish, and the Portuguese
In spring, summer, or in winter	In spring, summer, or winter (In spring, in summer, or in winter)

Correlative expressions (*both, and*; *not, but*; *not only, but also*; *either, or, first, second, third*; *and the like*) should be followed by the same grammatical construction. Many violations of this rule can be corrected by rearranging the sentence.

It was both a long ceremony and very tedious.	The ceremony was both long and tedious.
A time not for words, but action.	A time not for words, but for action.
Either you must grant his request or incur his ill will.	You must either grant his request or incur his ill will.
My objections are, first, the injustice of the measure; second, that it is unconstitutional.	My objections are, first, that the measure is unjust; second, that it is unconstitutional.

See also the third example under Rule 12 and the last under Rule 13.

It may be asked, what if a writer needs to express a rather large number of similar ideas, say twenty? Must he write twenty consecutive sentences of the same pattern? On closer examination he will probably find that the difficulty is imaginary, that his twenty ideas can be classified in groups, and that he need apply the principle only within each group. Otherwise, he had best avoid the difficulty by putting his statements in the form of a table.

16. Keep related words together.

The position of the words in a sentence is the principal means of showing their relationship. The writer must, therefore, so far as possible, bring together the words, and groups of words, that are related in thought, and keep apart those that are not so related.

The subject of a sentence and the principal verb should not, as a rule, be separated by a phrase or clause that can be transferred to the beginning.

Wordsworth, in the fifth book of *The Excursion*, gives a minute description of this church.	In the fifth book of *The Excursion*, Wordsworth gives a minute description of this church.

Cast iron, when treated in a Bessemer converter, is changed into steel.	By treatment in a Bessemer converter, cast iron is changed into steel.

The objection is that the interposed phrase or clause needlessly interrupts the natural order of the main clause. This objection, however, does not usually hold when the order is interrupted only by a relative clause or by an expression in apposition. Nor does it hold in periodic sentences in which the interruption is a deliberately used means of creating suspense (see examples under Rule 18).

The relative pronoun should come, as a rule, immediately after its antecedent.

There was a look in his eye that boded mischief.	In his eye was a look that boded mischief.
He wrote three articles about his adventures in Spain, which were published in *Harper's Magazine*.	He published in *Harper's Magazine* three articles about his adventures in Spain.
This is a portrait of Benjamin Harrison, grandson of William Henry Harrison, who became President in 1889.	This is a portrait of Benjamin Harrison, grandson of William Henry Harrison. He became President in 1889.

If the antecedent consists of a group of words, the relative comes at the end of the group, unless this would cause ambiguity.

The Superintendent of the Chicago Division, who	
A proposal to amend the Sherman Act, which has been variously judged	A proposal, which has been variously judged, to amend the Sherman Act
	A proposal to amend the much-debated Sherman Act
The grandson of William Henry Harrison, who	William Henry Harrison's grandson, Benjamin Harrison, who

A noun in apposition may come between antecedent and relative, because in such a combination no real ambiguity can arise.

> The Duke of York, his brother, who was regarded with hostility by the Whigs

Modifiers should come, if possible next to the word they modify. If several expressions modify the same word, they should be so arranged that no wrong relation is suggested.

All the members were not present.	Not all the members were present.
He only found two mistakes.	He found only two mistakes.
Major R. E. Joyce will give a lecture on Tuesday evening in Bailey Hall, to which the public is invited, on "My Experiences in Mesopotamia" at eight P.M.	On Tuesday evening at eight P.M., Major R. E. Joyce will give in Bailey Hall a lecture on "My Experiences in Mesopotamia." The public is invited.

17. In summaries, keep to one tense.

In summarizing the action of a drama, the writer should use the present tense. In summarizing a poem, story, or novel, he should preferably use the present tense. If the summary is in the present tense, antecedent action should be expressed by the perfect; if in the past, by the past perfect.

> An unforeseen chance prevents Friar John from delivering Friar Lawrence's letter to Romeo. Juliet, meanwhile, owing to her father's arbitrary change of the day set for her wedding, has been compelled to drink the potion on Tuesday night, with the result that Balthasar informs Romeo of her supposed death before Friar Lawrence learns of the nondelivery of the letter.

But whichever tense is used in the summary, a past tense in indirect discourse or in indirect question remains unchanged.

> The Legate inquires who struck the blow.

Apart from the exceptions noted, whichever tense the writer chooses, he should use throughout. Shifting from one tense to the other gives the appearance of uncertainty and irresolution (compare Rule 15).

In presenting the statements or the thought of someone else, as in summarizing an essay or reporting a speech, the writer should avoid intercalating such expressions as "he said," "he stated," "the speaker added," "the speaker then went on to say," "the author also thinks," or the like. He should indicate clearly at the outset, once for all, that what follows is summary, and then waste no words in repeating the notification.

In notebooks, in newspapers, in handbooks of literature, summaries of one kind or another may be indispensable, and for children in primary schools it is a useful exercise to retell a story in their own words. But in the criticism or interpretation of literature the writer should be careful to avoid dropping into summary. He may find it necessary to devote one or two sentences to indicating the subject, or the opening situation, of the work he is discussing; he may cite numerous details to illustrate its qualities. But he should aim to write an orderly discussion supported by evidence, not a summary with occasional comment. Similarly, if the scope of his discussion includes a number of works, he will as a rule do better not to take them up singly in chronological order, but to aim from the beginning at establishing general conclusions.

18. Place the emphatic words of a sentence at the end.

The proper place for the word, or group of words, which the writer desires to make most prominent is usually the end of the sentence.

Humanity has hardly advanced in fortitude since that time, though it has advanced in many other ways.	Humanity, since that time, has advanced in many other ways, but it has hardly advanced in fortitude.
This steel is principally used for making razors, because of its hardness.	Because of its hardness, this steel is principally used in making razors.

The word or group of words entitled to this position of prominence is usually the logical predicate, that is, the *new* element in the sentence, as it is in the second example.

The effectiveness of the periodic sentence arises from the prominence it gives to the main statement.

> Four centuries ago, Christopher Columbus, one of the Italian mariners whom the decline of their own republics had put at the service of the world and of adventure, seeking for Spain a westward passage to the Indies as a set-off against the achievements of Portuguese discoverers, lighted on America.

> With these hopes and in this belief I would urge you, laying aside all hindrance, thrusting away all private aims, to devote yourselves unswervingly and unflinchingly to the vigorous and successful prosecution of this war.

The other prominent position in the sentence is the beginning. Any element in the sentence, other than the subject, becomes emphatic when placed first.

> Deceit or treachery he could never forgive.

> So vast and rude, fretted by the action of nearly three thousand years, the fragments of this architecture may often seem, at first sight, like works of nature.

A subject coming first in its sentence may be emphatic, but hardly by its position alone. In the sentence,

> Great kings worshiped at his shrine,

the emphasis upon *kings* arises largely from its meaning and from the context. To receive special emphasis, the subject of a sentence must take the position of the predicate.

> Through the middle of the valley flowed a winding stream.

The principle that the proper place for what is to be made most prominent is the end applies equally to the words of a sentence, to the sentences of a paragraph, and to the paragraphs of a composition.

CHAPTER IV

A FEW MATTERS OF FORM

The few matters of form mentioned below were not an attempt to survey the entire field. They are intended merely to outline in brief the principal requirements of matters of form, with a focus on the fundamentals most commonly violated.

Headings. Leave a blank line, or its equivalent in space, after the title or heading of a manuscript. On succeeding pages, if using ruled paper, begin on the first line.

Numerals. Do not spell out dates or other serial numbers. Write them in figures or in Roman notation, as may be appropriate.

August 9, 1918	Chapter XII
Rule 3	352d Infantry

Exception: Spell out dates and numbers when they occur in speech.

"I arrived home on August ninth."

Parentheses. A sentence containing an expression in parenthesis is punctuated, outside of the marks of parenthesis, exactly as if the expression in parenthesis were absent. The expression within is punctuated as if it stood by itself, except that the final stop is omitted unless it is a question mark or an exclamation point.

> I went to his house yesterday (my third attempt to see him), but he had left town.

> He declares (and why should we doubt his good faith?) that he is now certain of success.

(When a wholly detached expression or sentence is parenthesized, the final stop comes before the last mark of parenthesis.)

Quotations. Formal quotations, cited as documentary evidence, are introduced by a colon and enclosed in quotation marks.

> The United States Coast Pilot has this to say of the place: "Bracy Cove, 0.5 mile eastward of Bear Island, is exposed to southeast winds, has a rocky and uneven bottom, and is unfit for anchorage."

A quotation grammatically in apposition or the direct object of a verb is preceded by a comma and enclosed in quotation marks.

> The provision of the Constitution is: "No tax or duty shall be laid on articles exported from any state"

Quotations grammatically in apposition or the direct objects of verbs are preceded by a comma and enclosed in quotation marks.

> I recall the maxim of La Rochefoucauld, "Gratitude is a lively sense of benefits to come."

> Aristotle says, "Art is an imitation of nature."

Quotations of an entire line, or more, of verse, are begun on a fresh line and centered, but not enclosed in quotation marks.

> Wordsworth's enthusiasm for the Revolution was at first unbounded:
>> Bliss was it in that dawn to be alive,
>> But to be young was very heaven!

Quotations introduced by *that* are regarded as in indirect discourse and not enclosed in quotation marks.

> Keats declares that beauty is truth, truth beauty.

Proverbial expressions and familiar phrases of literary origin require no quotation marks.

> These are the times that try men's souls.
>
> He lives far from the madding crowd.

The same is true of colloquialisms and slang.

References. In scholarly work requiring exact references, abbreviate titles that occur frequently, giving the full forms in an alphabetical list at the end. As a general practice, give the references in parenthesis or in footnotes, not in the body of the sentence. Omit the words *act, scene, line, book, volume, page,* except when referring by only one of them. Punctuate as indicated below.

In the second scene of the third act	In III.ii (still better, simply insert III.ii in parentheses at the proper place in the sentence)
After the killing of Polonius, Hamlet is placed under guard (IV. ii. 14).	
2 *Samuel* 1:17–27	Othello II.iii 264–267, III.iii. 155–161

Titles. For the titles of literary works, scholarly usage prefers italics with capitalized initials. The usage of editors and publishers varies, some using italics with capitalized initials, others using Roman with capitalized initials and with or without quotation marks. Use italics (indicated in manuscript by underscoring), except in writing for a periodical that follows a different practice. Omit initial *A* or *The* from titles when you place the possessive before them.

> *The Iliad; the Odyssey; As You Like It; To a Skylark; The Newcomers; A Tale of Two Cities; Dickens's Tale of Two Cities.*

CHAPTER V

WORDS AND EXPRESSIONS COMMONLY MISUSED

*"It's hard to imagine an engineer or manager who doesn't need to express himself in English prose as part of his job. It's also hard to imagine a writer who will not be improved by a liberal application of **The Elements of Style**."*
—*Telephone Engineer & Management*

Many of the words and expressions listed here are not so much examples of bad English as they are of bad style, typical of careless writing. As demonstrated in the section on "Feature," the proper correction often involves not merely replacing one word or set of words with another, but rather replacing vague generalities with precise statements.

All right. Idiomatic in familiar speech as a detached phrase in the sense, "Agreed," or "Go ahead." In other uses better avoided. Always written as two words.

As good or better than. Expressions of this type should be corrected by rearranging the sentence.

My opinion is as good or better than his.	My opinion is as good as his, or better (if not better).

As to whether. *Whether* is sufficient; see under Rule 13.

Bid. Takes the infinitive without *to*. The past tense is *bade*.

Case. The *Concise Oxford Dictionary* begins its definition of this word: "instance of a thing's occurring; usual state of affairs." In these two senses, the word is usually unnecessary.

In many cases, the rooms were poorly ventilated.	Many of the rooms were poorly ventilated.
It has rarely been the case that any mistake has been made.	Few mistakes have been made.

See Wood, *Suggestions to Authors*, pp. 68–71, and Quiller-Couch, *The Art of Writing*, pp. 103–106.

Certainly. Used indiscriminately by some speakers, much as others use *very*, to intensify any and every statement. A mannerism of this kind, bad in speech, is even worse in writing.

Character. Often simply redundant, used from a mere habit of wordiness.

Acts of a hostile character.	Hostile acts.

Claim, (verb). With object-noun, means *lay claim to*. May be used with a dependent clause if this sense is clearly involved: "He claimed that he was the sole surviving heir." (But even here, "claimed to be" would be better.) Not to be used as a substitute for *declare, maintain,* or *charge*.

Clever. This word has been greatly overused; it is best restricted to ingenuity displayed in small matters.

Compare. To *compare to* is to point out or imply resemblances, between objects regarded as essentially of different order; to *compare with* is mainly to point out differences, between objects regarded as essentially of the same order. Thus, life has been compared to a pilgrimage, to a drama, to a battle; Congress may be compared with the British Parliament. Paris has been compared to ancient Athens; it may be compared with modern London.

Consider. Not followed by *as* when it means, "believed to be." "I consider him thoroughly competent." Compare, "The lecturer considered Cromwell first as soldier and second as administrator," where "considered" means "examined" or "discussed."

Dependable. A needless substitute for *reliable, trustworthy.*

Due to. Incorrectly used for *through, because of,* or *owing to,* in adverbial phrases: "He lost the first game, due to carelessness." In correct use related as predicate or as modifier to a particular noun: "This invention is due to Edison"; "losses due to preventable fires."

Effect. As noun, means *result*; as verb, means *to bring about, accomplish* (not to be confused with *affect,* which means "to influence").

As noun, often loosely used in perfunctory writing about fashions, music, painting, and other arts: "an Oriental effect"; "effects in pale green"; "very delicate effects"; "broad effects"; "subtle effects"; "a charming effect was produced by." The writer who has a definite meaning to express will not take refuge in such vagueness.

Etc. Not to be used of persons. Equivalent to *and the rest, and so forth,* and hence not to be used if one of these would be insufficient, that is, if the reader would be left in doubt as to any important particulars. Least open to objection when it represents the last terms of a list already given in full, or immaterial words at the end of a quotation.

At the end of a list introduced by *such as, for example,* or any similar expression, *etc.* is incorrect.

Fact. Use this word only of matters of kind capable of direct verification, not of matters of judgment. That a particular event happened on a given date, that lead melts at a certain temperature, are facts. But such conclusions as that Napoleon was the greatest of modern generals, or that the climate of California is delightful, however incontestable they may be, are not properly facts.

On the formula *the fact that*, see under Rule 13.

Factor. A hackneyed word; the expressions of which it forms part can usually be replaced by something more direct and idiomatic.

His superior training was the great factor in his winning the match.	He won the match by being better trained.
Heavy artillery is becoming an increasingly important factor in deciding battles.	Heavy artillery is playing a larger and larger part in deciding battles.

Feature. Another hackneyed word; like *factor* it usually adds nothing to the sentence in which it occurs.

A feature of the entertainment especially worthy of mention was the singing of Miss. A.	(Better use the same number of words to tell what Miss A. sang, or if the program has already been given, to tell something of how she sang.)

As a verb, in the advertising sense of *offer as a special attraction*, to be avoided.

Fix. Colloquial in America for *arrange, prepare, mend.* In writing restrict it to its literary senses, *fasten, make firm or immovable*, etc.

He is a man who. A common type of redundant expression; see Rule 13.

He is a man who is very ambitious.	He is very ambitious.
Spain is a country which I have always wanted to visit.	I have always wanted to visit Spain.

However. In the meaning *nevertheless*, not to come first in its sentence or clause.

The roads were almost impassable. However, we at last succeeded in reaching camp.	The roads were almost impassable. At last, however, we succeeded in reaching camp.

When *however* comes first, it means *in whatever way* or *to whatever extent*.

However you advise him, he will probably do as he thinks best.
However discouraging the prospect, he never lost heart.

Kind of. Not to be used as a substitute for *rather* (before adjectives and verbs), or except in familiar style, for *something like* (before nouns). Restrict it to its literal sense: "Amber is a kind of fossil resin"; "I dislike that kind of notoriety." The same holds true of *sort of.*

Less. Should not be misused for *fewer*.

He had less men than in the previous campaign.	He had fewer men than in the previous campaign.

Less refers to quantity, *fewer* to number. "His troubles are less than mine" means "His troubles are not so great as mine." "His troubles are fewer than mine" means "His troubles are not so numerous as mine." It is, however, correct to say, "The signers of the petition were less than a hundred," where the round number, a hundred, is something like a collective noun, and *less* is thought of as meaning a less quality or amount.

Line, along these lines. *Line* in the sense of *course of procedure, conduct, thought*, is allowable, but has been so much overworked, particularly in the phrase *along these lines*, that a writer who aims at freshness or originality had better discard it entirely.

Mr. B. also spoke along the same lines.	Mr. B. also spoke, to the same effect.

He is studying along the line of French literature.	He is studying French literature.

Literal, literally. Often incorrectly used in support of exaggeration or violent metaphor.

A literal flood of abuse	A flood of abuse
Literally dead with fatigue	Almost dead with fatigue (dead tired)

Lose out. Meant to be more emphatic than *lose*, but actually less so, because of its commonness. The same holds true of *try out, win out, sign up, register up*. With a number of verbs, *out* and *up* form idiomatic combinations: *find out, run out, turn out, cheer up, dry up, make up*, and others, each distinguishable in meaning from the simple verb. *Lose out* is not.

Most. Not to be used for *almost*.

Most everybody	Almost everybody
Most all the time	Almost all the time

Nature. Often simply redundant, used like *character*.

Acts of a hostile nature	Hostile acts

Often vaguely used in such expressions as "a lover of nature"; "poems about nature." Unless more specific statements follow, the reader cannot tell whether the poems have to do with natural scenery, rural life, the sunset, the untracked wilderness, or the habits of squirrels.

Near by. Adverbial phrase not yet fully accepted as good English, though the analogy of *close by* and *hard by* seems to justify it. *Near*, or *near at hand*, is as good, if not better.

Not to be used as an adjective; use *neighboring*.

Oftentimes, ofttimes. Archaic forms, no longer in good use. The modern word is *often*.

One hundred and one. Retain the *and* in this and similar expressions, in accordance with the unvarying usage of English prose from Old English times.

One of the most. Avoid beginning essays or paragraphs with this formula, as, "One of the most interesting developments of modern science is, etc."; "Switzerland is one of the most interesting countries of Europe." There is nothing wrong in this; it is simply threadbare and forcible-feeble.

People. *The people* is a political term, not to be confused with *the public*. From the people comes political support or opposition; from the public comes artistic appreciation or commercial patronage.

The word *people* is not to be used with words of number, in place of *persons*. If of "six people" five went away, how many "people" would be left?

Phase. Means a stage of transition or development: "the phases of the moon"; "the last phase." Not to be used for *aspect* or *topic*.

Another phase of the subject	Another point (another question)

Possess. Not to be used as a mere substitute for *have* or *own*.

He possessed great courage.	He had great courage (was very brave).
He was the fortunate possessor of	He owned

Respective, respectively. These words may usually be omitted with advantage.

Works of fiction are listed under the names of their respective authors.	Works of fiction are listed under the names of their authors.

The one mile and two mile runs were won by Jones and Cummings respectively.	The one mile and two mile runs were won by Jones and by Cummings.

In some kinds of formal writing, as in geometrical proofs, it may be necessary to use *respectively*, but it should not appear in writing on ordinary subjects.

So. Avoid, in writing, the use of *so* as an intensifier: "so good"; "so warm"; "so delightful."

On the use of *so* to introduce clauses, see Rule 4.

Sort of. See under *Kind of.*

State. Not to be used as a mere substitute for *say*, *remark*. Restrict it to the sense of *express fully or clearly*, as, "He refused to state his objections."

Student body. A needless and awkward expression, meaning no more than the simple word *students*.

A member of the student body	A student
Popular with the student body	Liked by the students
The student body passed resolutions.	The students passed resolutions.

System. Frequently used without need.

Dayton has adopted the commission system of government.	Dayton has adopted government by commission.
The dormitory system	Dormitories

Thanking you in advance. This sounds as if the writer meant, "It will not be worth my while to write to you again." Simply write, "Thanking you," and if the favor which you have requested is granted, write a letter of acknowledgment.

They. A common inaccuracy is the use of the plural pronoun when the antecedent is a distributive expression such as *each, each one, everybody, every one, many a man*, which, though implying more than one person, requires the pronoun to be in the singular. Similar to this, but with even less justification, is the use of the plural pronoun with the antecedent *anybody, any one, somebody, some one*, the intention being either to avoid the awkward "he or she," or to avoid committing oneself to either. Some bashful speakers even say, "A friend of mine told me that they, etc."

Use *he* with all the above words, unless the antecedent is or must be feminine.

Very. Use this word sparingly. Where emphasis is necessary, use words strong in themselves.

Viewpoint. Write *point of view*, but do not misuse this, as many do, for *view* or *opinion.*

While. Avoid the indiscriminate use of this word for *and, but*, and *although.* Many writers use it frequently as a substitute for *and* or *but*, either from a mere desire to vary the connective, or from uncertainty which of the two connectives is the more appropriate. In this use it is best replaced by a semicolon.

The office and salesrooms are on the ground floor, while the rest of the building is devoted to manufacturing.	The office and salesrooms are on the ground floor; the rest of the building is devoted to manufacturing.

Its use as a virtual equivalent of *although* is allowable in sentences where this leads to no ambiguity or absurdity.

While I admire his energy, I wish it were employed in a better cause.

This is entirely correct, as shown by the paraphrase,

> I admire his energy; at the same time, I wish it were employed in a better cause.

Compare:

While the temperature reaches 90 or 95 degrees in the daytime, the nights are often chilly.	Although the temperature reaches 90 or 95 degrees in the daytime, the nights are often chilly.

The paraphrase,

> The temperature reaches 90 or 95 degrees in the daytime; at the same time the nights are often chilly,

shows why the use of *while* is incorrect.

In general, the writer will do well to use *while* only with strict literalness, in the sense of *during the time that*.

Whom. Often incorrectly used for *who* before *he said* or similar expressions, when it is really the subject of a following verb.

His brother, whom he said would send him the money	His brother, who he said would send him the money
The man whom he thought was his friend	The man who (that) he thought was his friend (whom he thought his friend)

Worth while. Overworked as a term of vague approval and (with *not*) of disapproval. Strictly applicable only to actions: "It is worth while to telegraph?"

His books are not worth while.	His books are not worth reading (not worth one's while to read; do not repay reading).

The use of *worth while* before a noun ("a worth while story") is indefensible.

Would. A conditional statement in the first person requires *should*, not *would*.

I should not have succeeded without his help.

The equivalent of *shall* in indirect quotation after a verb in the past tense is *should*, not *would*.

He predicted that before long we should have a great surprise.

To express habitual or repeated action, the past tense, without *would*, is usually sufficient, and from its brevity, more emphatic.

Once a year he would visit the old mansion.	Once a year he visited the old mansion.

CHAPTER VI

WORDS OFTEN MISSPELLED

"Every writer, by the way he uses the languages, reveals something of his spirit, his habits, his capacities, his bias. . . . Avoid the elaborate, the pretentious, the coy, and the cute. Do not be tempted by a twenty-dollar word when there is a ten-center handy, ready and able." —William Strunk, Jr.

A chapter often omitted in many editions of *The Elements of Style* by Strunk & White has been reintroduced here. We believe the work would not be complete without it. After all, Part 2, *The Elements of Style* by William Strunk, Jr., is designed to present the original, timeless work of Professor Strunk, which remains in the public domain. This section includes Professor Strunk's own list of the most commonly misspelled words in the English language.

In an era dominated by autocorrect and spellcheck, one might assume that spelling errors are a thing of the past. Yet, despite the advantages of modern technology, certain words continue to challenge us. To determine which words are most frequently misspelled, Strunk consulted several authoritative resources, including Merriam-Webster and the Oxford English Corpus—a database that helps Oxford English Dictionary editors track language usage. This meticulous research culminated in a definitive list by Strunk, illustrating the enduring complexity of English spelling. The complete list of these commonly misspelled words, as compiled by Strunk, is included herein.

Professor Strunk's Words Often Misspelled

accidentally	formerly	privilege
advice	humorous	pursue
affect	hypocrisy	repetition
beginning	immediately	rhyme
believe	incidentally	rhythm
benefit	latter	ridiculous
challenge	led	sacrilegious
criticize	lose	seize
deceive	marriage	separate
definite	mischief	shepherd
describe	murmur	siege
despise	necessary	similar
develop	occurred	simile
disappoint	parallel	too
duel	Philip	tragedy
ecstasy	playwright	tries
effect	preceding	undoubtedly
existence	prejudice	until
fiery	principal	

Previously, words like *to-day*, *to-night*, *to-morrow* were written with a hyphen. However, modern practice has eliminated the hyphens, and we now write *today*, *tonight*, and *tomorrow* as single words (AuthorsDoor commentary).

PART 3

AUTHORSDOOR
EDITORIAL STANDARDS
COMMENTARY

*"I shall have a word or two to say about attitudes in writing: the
how, the why, the beartraps, the power, and the glory."*
—E. B. White

Elwyn Brooks White (1899–1985) was an American writer renowned for his popular children's books, including *Stuart Little* (1945), *Charlotte's Web* (1952), and *The Trumpet of the Swan* (1970). In a 2012 survey conducted by *School Library Journal*, *Charlotte's Web* was voted the top children's novel in their poll of the top one hundred children's books. In addition to his literary achievements, White was a writer and contributing editor to *The New Yorker* magazine and co-authored the English language style guide, *The Elements of Style*.

E. B. White published his first article in *The New Yorker* in 1925, then joined the staff in 1927 and continued to contribute for nearly six decades. Best recognized for his essays and unsigned "Notes and Comment" pieces, he gradually became the magazine's most important contributor. Throughout his tenure at *The New Yorker*, he frequently provided "Newsbreaks"—short, witty comments on oddly worded printed items from many sources—under categories like "Block That Metaphor." He also served as a columnist for *Harper's Magazine* from 1938 to 1943.

In 1949, White published *Here Is New York*, a short book based on an article he had been commissioned to write for *Holiday* magazine. Editor Ted Patrick approached White about writing the essay, telling him it would be fun. "Writing is never 'fun'," replied White. That article reflects the writer's appreciation for a city that affords its residents both "the gift of loneliness and the gift of privacy." It concludes with a dark note touching on the forces that could destroy the city he loved. The prescient "love letter" to the city was re-published in 1999 on the centennial of his birth, with an introduction by his stepson, Roger Angell.

In 1959, E. B. White edited and updated *The Elements of Style*. This handbook of grammatical and stylistic guidance for writers of American English was first written by William Strunk, Jr., one of White's professors at Cornell, and published in 1918. White's reworking of the book was extremely well received, leading to later editions in 1972, 1979, and 2000. Maira Kalman illustrated an edition in 2005. That same year, a New York composer named Nico Muhly premiered a short opera based on the book. The volume has become a standard tool for students and writers and remains required reading in many composition classes. The complete history of *The Elements of Style* is detailed in Mark Garvey's *Stylized: A Slightly Obsessive History of Strunk & White's 'The Elements of Style'*.

In 1978, White won a special Pulitzer Prize citing "his letters, essays, and the full body of his work." He also received the Presidential Medal of Freedom in 1963 and honorary memberships in a variety of literary societies throughout the United States. The 1973 Oscar-nominated Canadian animated short *The Family That Dwelt Apart*, narrated by White, is based on his short story of the same name.

The "AuthorsDoor Edition: Elements of Style Revisited—The Writing Companion," PART 3—AuthorsDoor Editorial Standards Commentary, presents a modernized approach to style, replacing the original chapter by E. B. White in *The Elements of Style* by William Strunk, Jr., and E. B. White.

CHAPTER VII

STYLE CONSIDERATIONS AND TECHNIQUES

"White is one of the best stylists and most lucid minds in this country. What he says and his way of saying it are equally rewarding." —The Wall Street Journal

Diving into the realm of style, we're about to embark on an exhilarating journey, treading the thin line between the expected and the extraordinary. Until now, our "In-House Content Style Guide" has focused on the *rights* and *wrongs* of English, but as we venture into this final chapter, it's all about capturing that unique flair, that *je ne sais quoi*, which distinguishes the mundane from the magnificent.

It's a bit like asking why some melodies make our hearts soar while others, with just a few notes changed, barely register. There's no precise formula to this magic, no secret potion. And as tantalizing as it might sound, there isn't a straightforward guide to spellbinding writing either. Clear thinking doesn't always translate into lucid writing.

Picture this: writing, for many of us, feels like trying to catch lightning in a bottle. Our minds, those racing whirlwinds of ideas, always seem to be a few steps ahead of our pens. Imagine being an adventurer, where every writing expedition is about seizing those fleeting thoughts, much like a photographer captures a bird mid-flight.

As a writer, you're more of an explorer—sometimes lying in ambush in your favorite cozy nook, waiting for inspiration to saunter in; other times, you're on a quest, hunting down that elusive idea. Much like the thrill of the hunt, patience is the writer's best companion. Think of it: sometimes, it might take combing through a forest of thoughts just to find that one golden acorn.

So, dear reader, brace yourself! For the young and budding writer, navigating this chapter might feel like sailing vast seas, guided by stars that play hide and seek. It's thrilling, it's mysterious, and while there may not be a definite map, there's a world of wonder waiting to be discovered. Here are a few golden nuggets and pro-tips to help you weave your own captivating tapestry of words. Let the adventure begin!

1. The art of subtle storytelling.

Imagine being at a grand performance where the spotlight isn't on the performer, but on the mesmerizing dance or the soulful music. That's what your writing should aim for—where the author gracefully steps into the shadows, letting the story dance in the limelight.

Think of it this way: good writing is like a magic trick. When it's executed perfectly, the audience is so captivated by the illusion that they don't notice the magician. Your first golden rule? Keep it real and let go of pretense. Dive deep into the authentic rhythm of your words, and your unique style will naturally shimmer through. After all, it's YOU at the core of your stories.

And here's the secret sauce: as you hone your craft, not only will you carve out your niche, but you'll also find the magical bridge to connect with readers' hearts and minds. That's the ultimate goal and the sweetest reward of writing.

Remember, writing is both an art and a discipline. It challenges your thoughts and at the same time, enriches them. It's a cycle of emptying and filling, a beautiful dance of the mind that never grows old. So, take the pen, let your thoughts flow, and witness the magic unfold!

2. The dance of authentic writing.

Imagine writing as a dance to your favorite tune—it's all about moving to the rhythm that feels most organic to you. When you write your thoughts, let them flow as spontaneously as a conversation with a close friend. Use words that feel like home, the ones that come without hesitation.

But here's a little twist: just because your words flowed effortlessly doesn't mean they're pitch-perfect. Remember how, when we first started talking, we mimicked the sounds around us, soaking up words like sponges? As we grow, our linguistic repertoire does too, often mirroring the words and styles we adore.

So, should you shy away from echoing your favorite authors? Not at all! Just ensure you aren't copying them intentionally. Surround yourself with exceptional writing; let the beauty of good literature seep into your bones. This way, when you write from the heart, the essence of what's truly worth echoing will naturally reverberate through your words. So, dance to your own beat, but let the echoes of great rhythms inspire your steps!

3. Plotting the path.

Picture this: you're about to embark on a grand adventure. Would you dive in without a map or at least some idea of the landscape? Similarly, when crafting a piece of writing, having a rough blueprint in your mind can work wonders.

Think of it as the foundation for a magnificent building. Whether it's a skyscraper or a story, a design helps give it form and direction. That's not to say you always need a detailed plan sketched out. For instance, when jotting down a simple list of laundry items, you proceed item-by-item, much like checking off garments from a pile.

But imagine diving into a sprawling biography without any roadmap. It's like wandering through a dense forest without a compass; you'll likely get lost amid myriad details and facts, losing sight of the bigger narrative. So, whether you're weaving a short story or a grand epic, always have a sense of your journey's blueprint. It'll be your guiding star, ensuring your tale shines bright and true!

4. Creating masterpieces with words.

Think of writing as creating a vibrant painting. Nouns and verbs are your bold brushstrokes, the primary colors that breathe life into our canvas. Adjectives and adverbs? They're the delicate shades and tints, adding nuance but best used sparingly.

No shade or color can salvage a poorly drawn figure, just as no adjective can rescue a weak noun. That's not to say we don't love the flair of adjectives and adverbs—when used right, they can dazzle and transform a sentence. But by and large, it's the strength of nouns and verbs that truly makes your prose pop and sizzle. So, next time you're painting with words, let nouns and verbs be your star performers, and watch your masterpiece come alive!

5. Sculpting your story to perfection.

Imagine writing as sculpting a block of marble. Your first draft? That's just chipping away the excess, revealing a rough form. But to turn that form into a masterpiece, you need to carve, polish, and sometimes, start certain sections from scratch.

Every writer, no matter how seasoned, knows the dance of revision. Sometimes, it's a subtle shuffle of paragraphs; at other times, a dramatic overhaul. Think of your manuscript as a puzzle. Don't hesitate to shuffle the pieces, snip them, or even toss some out to see the bigger picture. And hey, if you go a snip too far, there's always the comforting thought that you can start afresh the next day.

Grab those scissors and be fearless in your revisions. It's not a mark of your manuscript's frailty, but rather the refining fire through which all great writing must pass. Embrace it, and remember, every revision is a step closer to brilliance!

6. Finding the perfect writing recipe.

Think of writing as preparing a gourmet meal. Overwriting is like over-seasoning—while a dash of spice can elevate a dish, too much can overwhelm the palate and mask the true flavors. Writing that's overly ornate or flamboyant is akin to a dish dripping with excess sauce; it becomes hard to savor and can leave the reader feeling full before they've truly tasted the essence of your message.

A balance is essential. Just as a chef knows the importance of letting the natural flavors of ingredients shine, a writer should aim for clarity and simplicity. It's okay to sprinkle in some rich descriptions or fancy words here and there, but moderation is key. After all, you want your readers to leave satisfied, not overwhelmed by a buffet of extravagance. So in the kitchen of composition, remember: less is often more, and the best flavors are often the simplest.

7. Crafting credible narratives.

Picture this: writing is like weaving a delicate fabric of trust with your reader. Now, imagine spilling a big blot of ink on it—that's overstatement. The moment you exaggerate, it's like sounding an alarm, making your reader pull back, skeptical of every thread you've woven.

It's like inviting someone to marvel at a magical landscape, but then pointing out a mountain and calling it "the tallest in the universe." That one lofty claim can overshadow the genuine beauty around it. The reader, once entranced, now raises an eyebrow, questioning not just the height of the mountain, but the authenticity of the entire vista.

It's tempting to amplify for effect, but the cost can be trust. Keep your narrative genuine, for even a momentary lapse into the realm of exaggeration can cast a long shadow over your tale's credibility. So, tread carefully and let the true magic of your words shine through!

8. Crafting clearer narratives without qualifiers.

Imagine your writing is a clear, sparkling lake. Now picture qualifiers like "rather," "very," "little," and "pretty" as pesky little critters muddying those pristine waters. These wordy critters tend to latch onto your prose, dimming the vibrancy of your language.

Consider the word "little." It's a sneaky one! Outside of indicating size, it often dilutes the power of a statement. It's akin to pouring water into a flavorful drink—the essence gets lost. Let's make a pact: let's sharpen our writing, keep an eagle eye on these qualifiers, and ensure they don't gatecrash our prose party too often. Because, believe it or not, removing these little intruders can make a "pretty" big difference to the clarity and punch of our writing! Dive in and make those words sparkle!

9. Perfecting your writing tone.

Imagine writing as a gentle sailboat ride. Now, while a gust of wind might make things exciting momentarily, a perpetual, strong breeze could tip the boat over. Similarly, in writing, adopting a persistently breezy, over-the-top style can make your prose feel like it's teetering on the edge.

In today's era of abundant writing, it's easy to spot content that seems as if the writer had one too many cups of caffeine. Sure, Walt Whitman celebrated the "spontaneous self," but let's not mistake unbridled enthusiasm for genuine insight. It's like assuming every photobomb is a masterpiece.

In essence, a constantly breezy style might give the impression of someone a tad too in love with their own voice, assuming every thought they have is a gem. So, let's not let our prose get swept away in a gust. Instead, strive for authenticity, balance, and true connection with the reader. Smooth sailing!

10. Picking the timeless over trendy in spelling.

Think of writing as dressing up for an important event. While it's fun to experiment with fashion, there are times when classic and timeless attire is the way to go. Similarly, in the world of words, sticking to conventional spelling is like donning that classic outfit.

Imagine texting a friend and saying "nite" instead of "night" or "thru" instead of "through." While it might be quirky in a casual setting, in formal writing, it's akin to wearing sneakers to a black-tie event. Unless you're setting a whole new trend and ready to face the raised eyebrows, it's best to stick to the traditional.

In short, while there's a time and place for creative spelling, most writing occasions call for the elegance of tradition. So, when in doubt, dress your prose in its timeless best!

11. Trusting dialogue to tell the tale.

Picture writing as crafting a suspenseful movie. Now, imagine a director giving away all the plot twists in the first ten minutes. Not very thrilling, right? Similarly, in writing, there's an art to leaving some things unsaid, letting the narrative unfold and the readers connect the dots.

Take dialogue, for instance. It's like watching two actors on a stage. If their conversation is genuine, you won't need a narrator constantly chiming in with "he said sadly" or "she replied excitedly." The dialogue itself, the raw emotion and rhythm of the words, should paint the picture.

Sometimes, budding writers sprinkle their dialogues with a dash too many adverbs or switch up simple "said" with fancier verbs. It's as if they're adding neon signs to their prose saying, "Look here! Feel this!" But true magic lies in subtlety. The trick? Trust your dialogue to convey the mood and trust your reader to catch the nuance. After all, less is often more, especially when it allows imagination to take the lead!

12. Mixing the right ingredients.

Imagine crafting words as if you're whipping up a delicious smoothie. While it's tempting to throw in every ingredient at hand, sometimes that results in a weird, unpalatable mix. Crafting adverbs is similar. Sure, slap on an "ly" to an adjective, and voila, you have an adverb. But, is it always a tasty choice?

Consider the concoction "tangledly." It feels like trying to sip a smoothie with too many chunky bits. Or "tiredly," which, though it might seem fine, doesn't roll off the tongue in everyday chatter.

The secret sauce? Stick to the ingredients—or in this case, words—that people relish in daily conversation. If it sounds odd out loud, it might just stick out on paper. So, blend wisely, and serve up prose that's both delightful and easy to digest!

13. Directing dialogue with precision.

Imagine diving into a book, getting lost in an engrossing conversation between characters, only to realize . . . wait, who just said that? Dialogue, without clear signposts, is like watching a play with all actors behind a curtain. You hear the voices, but you're left guessing who's who.

When you dive into the world of dialogue, it's essential to leave breadcrumbs for your reader. If you lead them down a long conversation with no clear markers, they might end up retracing their steps, and that's like making them rewatch a movie scene because they missed the plot. Not the best experience, right?

And hey, while attributives like "he said" or "she replied" are your guiding stars, make sure they don't stumble into the conversation and trip up the flow. Think of them as subtle stage directions. If you're ever in doubt about where to place them, just voice out the dialogue. Let the natural pauses guide you, ensuring the reader enjoys a seamless performance. After all, clarity is the ultimate showstopper!

14. Styling sentences for the occasion.

Think of words as wardrobe choices. Just as you wouldn't wear a tuxedo to a beach party, don't reach for grandiose words when simpler ones will do the trick. Why strut in high heels when comfy sneakers fit the occasion perfectly? Remember, while "resplendent" might sound exquisite, sometimes "shiny" captures the essence just right.

Our language has its roots, with snappy Anglo-Saxon words often packing more punch than their Latin counterparts. Compare "gut" to "intestine." Sure, "gut" has that raw, visceral sound, but it won't always fit the mood. Just like you wouldn't casually call a stomach a "tummy" in a medical journal.

The boundary between overly ornate and the refreshingly clear can be as thin as a razor's edge. It all boils down to having a good ear. It's your secret weapon in the world of writing. Just like a musician knows when a note is off, a writer with a tuned ear knows when to ditch formality for a splash of colloquial charm or when to play by the grammar rules. So, keep your ears perked up. Let them be your compass, guiding you through the symphony of words, helping you hit the right notes every time!

15. More than just words, it's a dance.

Imagine trying to mimic a dance from a culture different than your own. If you don't get the steps just right, you might come off as inauthentic or even disrespectful. Similarly, playing with dialect in writing is a delicate dance. Unless you've truly grooved to its rhythm, it's easy to miss a step.

Dialect isn't just about sprinkling a few quirky words here and there. It's about capturing the very essence of a language, its nuances, its cadence. For instance, take the word "once." You might be tempted to spell it "oncet" in dialect, but that could read like "onset." Perhaps "wunst" would be a closer match. But remember, consistency is key! If you twirl one way at the beginning, make sure to keep twirling the same way throughout.

Top-notch dialect writers are like skilled dancers; they don't overdo their moves. They capture the essence with subtlety, ensuring the reader feels the rhythm without getting overwhelmed. So, if you decide to dance the dialect dance, make sure to do so with finesse and respect for its original beauty!

16. Striving for clarity in every sentence.

Imagine writing as building a crystal-clear windowpane. What good is a window if it's murky or foggy, blocking the view? Your primary mission? Keep it clear, so clear that the reader can see right through the heart of your message.

Ever felt like you're wrestling with a sentence, trapped in a twisty maze of words? Don't push against the thicket. Sometimes, it's best to take a step back and carve a new path. Maybe that winding sentence can be split into two breezy ones, or perhaps a few excess words are clouding the view.

Unclear prose isn't just a hiccup; it can lead to grand misunderstandings. It's like sending someone on a treasure hunt but forgetting the map. So, whenever you lay down your words, ensure they shine with clarity. After all, in the theater of writing, clarity is the star that steals the show!

17. Serving up relevance over ego.

Imagine writing as hosting a dinner party. While it's a great platform to showcase your culinary skills, it's probably not the best time to share your strong views on, say, pineapple on pizza. Just like with food, when it comes to writing, it's key to know when to serve your opinions and when to keep them on the back burner.

We all have a treasure trove of opinions, and oh, how tempting it is to sprinkle them into our prose! But, dishing them out without a good reason can come off as assuming everyone's hungry for them. And let's face it, a piece peppered with unsolicited views might leave behind a whiff of ego.

Let's say you're invited to speak at a new cat café opening, but you're more of a dog person. In your polite decline, there's no need to launch into a tirade about feline foes. Keep it classy, keep it relevant. Remember, they wanted your voice, not necessarily your views on cats versus dogs. In writing, as in hosting, knowing what to serve and when makes all the difference!

18. The dos and don'ts of flavorful writing.

Imagine your writing as a seasoning cabinet. Figures of speech are those exotic spices that can turn a simple dish into a culinary delight. But what happens when you toss in too much saffron, followed by a dash of truffle oil, then a sprinkle of star anise? Your readers, or in this case, taste-testers, might be left overwhelmed, trying to decipher the explosion of flavors.

It's like being at a fireworks show where every firework goes off at once—dazzling, sure, but also chaotic. Readers need a moment to savor each simile, to revel in its beauty. If they're always jumping from one comparison to another, they might end up feeling more like they're on a wild goose chase than on a delightful journey.

And let's talk about mixed metaphors. It's like starting a story in a deep-sea dive with swordfish and suddenly shifting to a desert with hourglasses. A tad disorienting, right? So, as you sprinkle in those figures of speech, remember: a pinch here and there enhances the flavor, but a heavy hand can leave things tasting a bit off!

19. Guiding readers through the forest of acronyms.

Picture writing as mapping out a treasure hunt. While shortcuts can make the journey quick, if they lead to confusion, your readers might end up lost in the woods, missing the treasure altogether.

Initials can be like secret paths known only to the locals. For instance, not everyone might recognize that "N.A.A.C.P." stands for the National Association of the Advancement of Colored People. And even if seasoned explorers are familiar, newcomers might be scratching their heads.

Think about the future generations of treasure hunters—the young adventurers stepping onto the trail for the first time. They deserve clear signposts, not cryptic symbols. A savvy move? Start with the full name, like laying down the base of the map. Once your readers have their compass set, you can lead them through shortcuts. That way, everyone's on the same adventurous page, finding the treasure with glee!

20. The risks and rewards of multilingual writing.

Imagine writing as hosting an international potluck dinner. While it's exciting to introduce guests to exotic flavors from around the globe, serving dish after dish from different cuisines might leave them craving a comforting, familiar taste.

Dabbling in other languages can add a dash of flair to your prose, a sprinkle of worldly charm. But, going overboard? It can be like serving your guests a five-course French meal when they came expecting good ol' comfort food. Some writers, in their zest to dazzle, garnish their pages with a medley of foreign phrases, often leaving readers feeling like they've bitten into something they can't quite chew.

The key is balance. A sprinkle of international flavor can be delightful, but make sure the main course remains relatable and digestible. After all, when your readers sit down to feast on your words, you want them to leave satisfied, not reaching for a translation menu. Bon appétit—or better yet, enjoy your meal!

21. Navigating the marketplace of language.

Think of language as a bustling city marketplace. There are well-trodden main streets, familiar and comfortable. Then, there are those intriguing alleyways—offbeat, eccentric, each humming to its own unique rhythm. As a writer, you're a traveler in this marketplace, captivated by every corner.

From the catchy jingles of the Advertising Avenue, with its playful twist on words, to the structured dialogues in Business Boulevard or the intricate lingo lanes of Law and Government Gardens, there are countless dialects and jargons to explore. The language landscape is ever-evolving, like a river, constantly reshaped by incoming streams of slang, industry jargon, and cultural nuances.

But here's the thing: while those quirky alleyways are fun to explore, the main streets have stood the test of time for a reason. They're familiar to everyone. Writing in standard language might seem like sticking to the main road, but navigating it is an adventure in itself. So, while it's great to be inspired by the many dialects of our vast language city, it's equally vital to master the art of walking the main streets with confidence and flair. Adventure awaits at every linguistic turn!

Imagine writing as being a chef. Your style? It's not just about the ingredients or the method, but about the passion, intuition, and personal flair you infuse into every dish. As a wise culinary master once put it, "Cooking isn't about following a recipe to the letter, but the joy of creating."

This cookbook frequently mentions "the diner." It's vital to appreciate the diner's tastes, but pandering exclusively to them is a slippery slope. Cook primarily for yourself. If you're always looking over your shoulder, trying to anticipate the next food trend or what diners might crave, you risk losing the essence of your unique culinary voice—even if it means having a packed restaurant every night.

Loaded with passion and guided by age-old cooking rules, the chef is ready to serve. It's like being the fearless cow in the old rhyme by Robert Louis Stevenson—buffeted by winds, drenched in rains, yet standing tall and undeterred. In today's terms, she's totally embracing the elements. Thanks to Stevenson's poetic touch, this one cow, amongst countless others, became iconic. Just like that steadfast chef or writer, she remains timeless, unswayed by passing storms. Her story will be savored for generations. So, write or cook with your heart, and let the world feast on your creations!

FURTHER READING

American Psychological Association. *The Publication Manual of the American Psychological Association, 6th Edition.*

Associated Press. *The Associated Press Stylebook, 55th Edition.* Dayton, Ohio: Lorenz Publishing Company, 2020.

Bernstein, Theodore M. *The Careful Writer: A Modern Guide to English Usage.* New York: The Free Press, 1965.

Collins, Frederick Howard. *Author and Printer.* London: Henry Frowde, 1905.

Collins, Frederick Howard, *Authors' and Printers' Dictionary.* London: Henry Frowde, 1912.

De Vinne, Theodore Low. *The Printers' Price List.* New York: Francis Hart and Company, 1871.

De Vinne, Theodore Low. *The Invention of Printing: A Collection of Facts and Opinions.* New York: Francis Hart and Company, 1876.

De Vinne, Theodore Low. *Historic Printing Types — The Practice of Typography.* New York: The Century Co., 1886.

De Vinne, Theodore Low. *Plain Printing Types — The Practice of Typography, Vol. 1.* New York: The Century Co., 1900.

De Vinne, Theodore Low. *Correct Composition — The Practice of Typography, Vol. 2.* New York: The Century Company, 1901.

De Vinne, Theodore Low. *The Treatise on Title-Pages — The Practice of Typography, Vol. 3.* New York: The Century Company, 1902.

De Vinne, Theodore Low. *Modern Methods of Book Composition — The Practice of Typography, Vol. 4.* New York: The Century Company, 1904.

De Vinne, Theodore Low. *Notable Printers of Italy during the Fifteenth Century*. New York: The Grolier Club, 1910.

Follett, Wilson and Wensberg, Erik. *Modern American Usage: A Guide by Wilson Follett and Erik Wensberg*. New York: Hill and Wang, 1979.

Fowler, Henry Watson. *The New Fowler's Modern English Usage, Third Edition, edited by R.W. Burchfield*. Oxford: Oxford University Press, 2004.

Hall, John Lesslie. *English Usage: Studies in the History and Uses of English Words and Phrases*. New York: Scott, Foresman and Company, 1917.

Hart, Horace. *Rules for Compositors and Printers*. London: Oxford University Press, 1893.

Hart, Horace. *Rules for Compositors and Readers*. London: Oxford University Press, 1905.

Kelly, James P. *Workmanship in Words*. Boston: Little, Brown and Co., 1916.

Lounsbury, Thomas Raynesford. *A History of the English Language*. New York: Henry Holt and Company, 1879.

Lounsbury, Thomas Raynesford. *Life of James Fenimore Cooper*. New York: Henry Holt and Company, 1882.

Lounsbury, Thomas Raynesford. *Studies in Chaucer, Three Volumes*. New York: Henry Holt and Company, 1891.

Lounsbury, Thomas Raynesford. *Shakespeare as a Dramatic Artist*. New York: Charles Scribner's Sons, 1901.

Lounsbury, Thomas Raynesford. *Shakespeare and Voltaire*. New York: Charles Scribner's Sons, 1902.

Lounsbury, Thomas Raynesford. *The Standard of Pronunciation in English*. New York and London: Harper & Brothers Publishers, 1904.

Lounsbury, Thomas Raynesford. *The Text of Shakespeare*. New York: Charles Scribner's Sons, 1906.

Lounsbury, Thomas Raynesford. *The Standard of Usage in English*. New York and London: Harper & Brothers Publishers, 1908.

Lounsbury, Thomas Raynesford. *English Spelling and Spelling Reform*. New York and London: Harper & Brothers Publishers, 1909.

Lounsbury, Thomas Raynesford. *Shakespeare as a Dramatic Artist: With an Account of His Reputation at Various Periods*. New York: Charles Scribner's Sons, 1912.

Merriam-Webster, Incorporated. *Merriam-Webster's Collegiate Dictionary, Eleventh Edition*. Springfield, Massachusetts: Merriam-Webster, 2003.

Merriam-Webster, Incorporated. *Webster's Third New International Dictionary of the English Language*. Springfield, Massachusetts: Merriam-Webster, 2002.

Modern Language Association of America. *The MLA Handbook, 8th Edition*. New York: Modern Language Association of America, 2016.

Modern Language Association. *The MLA Style Manual and Guide to Scholarly Publishing, 3rd Edition*. New York: Modern Language Association of America, 2016.

Quiller-Couch, Sir Arthur. *On the Art of Writing*. New York: G. P. Putnam's Sons, 1921.

Quiller-Couch, Sir Arthur. *The Oxford Book of English Verse*. Oxford: Clarendon Press, 1900.

Strunk, Jr., William. *The Elements of Style*. Ithaca, New York: Privately printed by Professor Strunk, 1918, published by Harcourt in 1920.

Strunk, Jr., William & E. B. White. *The Elements of Style, 4th Edition*. Britain: Macmillan Publishing Co., Inc., 1959, 1972, 1979.

Turabian, Kate Larimore. *A Manual for Writers of Research Papers, Theses, and Dissertations*. Chicago: University of Chicago Press, 1937.

University of Chicago. *The Chicago Manual of Style, 17th Edition*. Chicago: University of Chicago Press, 2017.

University of Michigan. *The American Heritage Dictionary of the English Language, Third Edition*. Boston: Houghton Mifflin, 1992.

Wood, George McLane. *Extracts from the Style Book of the Government Printing Office*. Washington, D.C.: Government Printing Office, 1915.

Wood, George McLane. *Suggestions to Authors*. Washington, D.C.: Government Printing Office, 1913.

RESOURCES

In the digital age, a plethora of tools and platforms aid in enhancing the writing and collaborative process. Grammar checkers like Grammarly, ProWritingAid, and the Hemingway App ensure linguistic accuracy. Comprehensive writing environments such as Scrivener, Ulysses, and Novlr provide structured canvases for writers. Evernote and Microsoft OneNote offer powerful platforms for research and note-taking. The journey from manuscript to published work is streamlined by tools like Vellum and the Reedsy Book Editor, with Sigil catering specifically to e-book creators. Emphasizing distraction-free creativity, FocusWriter and OmmWriter offer minimalist writing spaces, while collaborative platforms such as Google Docs and Dropbox Paper enable real-time teamwork. Visual thinkers benefit from mind mapping tools like Scapple and Plottr. In the backdrop of all digital endeavors, Backupery for Scrivener ensures data protection for writers, and Git offers robust version control for varied professionals. Together, these tools and platforms encompass the modern digital toolkit, enhancing productivity, creativity, and collaboration.

Grammar and Style Checkers

In today's digital age, where writing is an integral part of communication, maintaining accuracy and clarity has never been more important. Grammar and style checkers are invaluable tools designed to assist writers in presenting their ideas fluently and error-free. These software solutions analyze text for common grammatical mistakes, stylistic inconsistencies, and even nuanced tone mishaps. They ensure that every piece of writing—from professional reports to personal emails—upholds the highest standards of language precision. Their growing popularity underscores a universal desire: to communicate effectively and leave a lasting impression on readers.

Grammarly

Since its conception, Grammarly has quickly risen to prominence as one of the premier digital writing assistants in the market. Harnessing the power of advanced algorithms and artificial intelligence (AI), it corrects not only basic grammatical and spelling errors but also offers insights into clarity, tone, and stylistic improvements. Grammarly integrates seamlessly with browsers, word processors, and other platforms, providing real-time feedback. This empowers writers of all proficiency levels—from students to professionals—to produce polished, professional-quality content. As the realm of digital communication continues to expand, tools like Grammarly play a pivotal role in ensuring clarity and coherence in our daily interactions.

ProWritingAid

In the landscape of digital writing tools, ProWritingAid stands out as a comprehensive writing companion designed for those who aspire to elevate their prose. Beyond the capabilities of a typical grammar checker, it delves into the intricacies of style, structure, and readability, offering tailored suggestions that transform good writing into great writing. With its suite of detailed reports and analyses, ProWritingAid serves not just as a corrective tool but as an educational platform that guides users toward a deeper understanding of the craft. For writers, editors, and professionals alike, it offers a valuable lens through which they can refine their voice and communicate with precision.

Hemingway App

The Hemingway App, named in homage to the iconic American author known for his concise and clear prose, is a testament to the power of simplicity in writing. This innovative tool goes beyond mere grammar checks, focusing on enhancing the readability and impact of text. By highlighting long sentences, passive voice usage, and unnecessary adverbs, it nudges writers towards a style that is direct and unambiguous. In an age overwhelmed by information, the Hemingway App champions the idea that clear, straightforward communication is key to effective storytelling and understanding.

WhiteSmoke

WhiteSmoke has emerged as a multifaceted tool in the world of digital writing assistance, addressing not only grammar and style but also offering translation capabilities spanning over 50 languages. Its comprehensive approach to writing improvement encompasses spelling, punctuation, and stylistic suggestions, ensuring that users present their ideas with clarity and finesse. Moreover, with its integrated translation feature, WhiteSmoke bridges linguistic barriers, making it an indispensable asset for global communicators. Whether you're penning a business report or translating a document, WhiteSmoke provides a robust platform to enhance and diversify your written communication.

Writing Environments and Organizers

In the vast realm of writing, where ideas flow and narratives intertwine, the importance of structured spaces cannot be overstated. Writing environments and organizers serve as the backbone for authors, providing a cohesive framework to channel creativity and maintain focus. Tailored to accommodate the multifaceted nature of writing projects, these tools offer more than just word processing capabilities. They facilitate the organization of thoughts, plots, and research, creating a harmonious workspace where writers can seamlessly transition from brainstorming to drafting. As writing projects grow in complexity, these specialized environments become essential allies, ensuring that every thought finds its rightful place on the page.

Scrivener

Scrivener, more than just a word processor, is a sanctuary for writers who delve into lengthy and intricate projects. Tailored specifically for novelists, screenwriters, and researchers, this software offers a dynamic environment where ideas can be organized, plotted, and refined with unparalleled ease. Its unique interface allows users to break down their work into chapters, scenes, or research notes, revolutionizing the writing process by providing a visual roadmap of one's narrative or argument through tools like corkboard views and outliners. In an industry where structure is paramount, Scrivener stands as a beacon, offering writers both the flexibility to experiment and the structure to consolidate.

Ulysses

Ulysses, with its minimalist design and powerful capabilities, redefines the essence of a focused writing environment. Tailored for both seasoned authors and casual writers, this software for Mac and iOS platforms champions the principle of distraction-free writing. Its clean and intuitive interface, paired with organizational prowess, allows writers to fully immerse themselves in their craft, navigating seamlessly from one thought to the next. In the age where attention is a coveted commodity, Ulysses offers a serene oasis, ensuring that each word is penned with undisturbed contemplation.

Novlr

In the constellation of digital writing platforms, Novlr shines brightly as a beacon for novelists seeking both simplicity and functionality. Crafted with the unique needs of storytellers in mind, this online platform offers an intuitive environment that seamlessly blends chapter organization with a distraction-free writing space. As the narrative unfolds, authors can effortlessly navigate their story's structure, ensuring a coherent and well-paced flow. Featuring a user-centric design that adapts to individual writing styles and cloud-based capabilities that ensure work is accessible and secure across multiple devices, Novlr is not just a tool—it's a companion for every writer's journey from the first word to the final draft.

yWriter

In the realm of writing software tailored for authors, yWriter stands out with its meticulous approach to structuring narrative works. Designed specifically for novelists, it offers a compartmentalized environment where stories can be broken down into chapters and scenes. This structure allows writers to manage their narratives at both macro and micro levels, providing invaluable insights into pacing, character development, and plot progression. Free from the clutter of superfluous features, yWriter provides a focused space where storytellers can breathe life into their visions, one scene at a time, setting it apart from less specialized tools.

Research and Note-taking

In the intricate dance of knowledge acquisition and idea generation, research and note-taking play pivotal roles. These intertwined processes serve as the backbone of intellectual exploration, enabling thinkers, students, and professionals to distill vast amounts of information into coherent and accessible insights. Whether penning a scholarly article, planning a novel, or diving deep into a new subject of interest, the art of jotting down key points and organizing them systematically proves invaluable. In this age of information overload, effective research and note-taking are more than just academic skills; they are essential tools for clarity, understanding, and innovation.

Evernote

Evernote stands as a titan of organization and information management in the digital landscape of productivity tools. Born from the need to capture thoughts, save online discoveries, and streamline research, it has evolved into a versatile platform where notes, images, and documents converge into easily accessible notebooks. Whether you're a student consolidating study materials, a professional organizing details of projects, or a writer collecting snippets of inspiration, Evernote serves as a dynamic digital workspace. Its ability to synchronize across devices ensures that, no matter where you are, your ideas and findings are always within arm's reach.

Microsoft OneNote

In the realm of digital note-taking solutions, Microsoft OneNote emerges as a dynamic and versatile powerhouse. Seamlessly integrating the familiarity of traditional notebooks with the benefits of digital innovation, OneNote offers users an expansive canvas where text, drawings, and multimedia coexist in harmony. Its flexible structure allows for free-form input and hierarchical organization, catering to a diverse range of needs—from academic research and project planning to daily to-dos and creative brainstorming. Backed by the robustness of Microsoft's ecosystem, OneNote not only promises a repository for ideas but also a collaborative space where thoughts evolve and crystallize.

Formatting and Publishing

In the journey from conception to completion of a literary work, the steps of formatting and publishing represent both a culmination of the creative process and a new beginning for the work's public life. These processes transform raw manuscripts into polished pieces, ready for readers' eyes. Formatting ensures that the content adheres to specific aesthetic and structural norms, such as consistent typography and appropriate margins, providing a seamless reading experience. Publishing, on the other hand, is the gateway that introduces the work to the world, whether through traditional publishing houses or modern self-publishing platforms. In an era where content is king, mastering the art and science of formatting and publishing is paramount for any writer seeking to leave a lasting impact on their audience.

Vellum

Amidst the plethora of tools catering to writers and self-publishers, Vellum emerges as a model of elegance and efficiency. Exclusively crafted for the Mac ecosystem, this software transcends traditional book formatting limitations, offering authors a streamlined process to bring their manuscripts to life. With intuitive design controls and a suite of sophisticated templates, Vellum ensures that both e-books and print editions resonate with professional quality. As the self-publishing landscape continues to evolve, Vellum stands as a testament to the belief that every story, regardless of its origin, deserves a presentation that matches its essence.

Reedsy Book Editor

In the dynamic world of self-publishing, where authors take the reins of both writing and production, tools like the Reedsy Book Editor have become indispensable. Bridging the gap between raw manuscript and professionally crafted book, this online platform offers a blend of simplicity and sophistication. Thanks to its user-friendly interface, authors can effortlessly format their works for both print and digital mediums, adhering to the high-quality standards expected in the industry. As the lines between traditional and independent publishing blur, the Reedsy Book Editor stands as a beacon for authors, ensuring that their voice reaches readers in its most polished form.

Sigil

Delving into the world of e-book creation, Sigil stands out as a robust, open-source editor tailored for the EPUB format. Beyond the mere task of text editing, Sigil provides a comprehensive environment where authors and publishers can craft, structure, and fine-tune their digital books. With features that cater to both novice users and seasoned developers, it strikes a balance between flexibility and user-friendliness. As e-books continue to carve a significant niche in the literary landscape, tools like Sigil play a pivotal role in democratizing the publishing process, ensuring that stories are told with both clarity and technical precision.

Distraction-Free Writing

In an era inundated with notifications, digital distractions, and incessant multitasking, the quest for focused creativity has birthed the concept of distraction-free writing. This minimalist approach strips away the superfluous elements of traditional word processors, offering writers a serene canvas where thoughts can flow unimpeded. Rather than battling pop-ups or sifting through complex toolbars, authors find themselves immersed in a space where the written word takes center stage. As our digital environment becomes ever more clamorous, the allure of distraction-free writing grows, promising a sanctuary where ideas can flourish in their purest form.

FocusWriter

In the realm of minimalist writing tools, FocusWriter stands out as a beacon of simplicity and immersion. Designed to shield writers from the bustling digital distractions of modern computing, this software offers an uncluttered canvas that envelops the user in a world where only words matter. With its customizable themes, timers, and daily goals, FocusWriter goes beyond mere word processing; it crafts an environment tailored to the rhythms and needs of individual writers, enhancing productivity and focus. For those seeking a haven where creativity can flow without interruption, FocusWriter emerges as a cherished companion in the literary journey.

WriteMonkey

Amid the panorama of writing tools that prioritize simplicity, WriteMonkey holds a distinct position with its zen-like approach to the craft of writing. Boasting a stripped-down, clutter-free interface, it offers writers an enclave of concentration, free from the bells and whistle of conventional word processors. But don't be deceived by its minimalist facade; beneath it lies a suite of powerful features that cater to the needs of the modern writer. For those who yearn for a digital space that mimics the intimacy of pen and paper, WriteMonkey stands as a testament to the beauty of undisturbed creativity.

OmmWriter

In the tapestry of digital writing environments, OmmWriter weaves a unique narrative of serenity and focus. Distinguished by its ambient soundscapes and tranquil backgrounds, this software transcends traditional writing platforms by offering an immersive experience that taps into the senses. It's not just about penning words; it's about crafting them in a meditative space designed to nurture both mind and soul. As writers increasingly seek refuge from the noise of modern life, OmmWriter emerges as a haven, celebrating the harmonious union of thought, sound, and vision.

Collaboration

In the symphony of progress and innovation, collaboration emerges as the harmonizing force that amplifies individual talents and bridges disparate ideas. It is the crucible within which diverse perspectives meld, birthing solutions that no single mind could conceive alone. Whether in the realms of business, art, or academia, collaboration transcends mere cooperation, fostering a space where creativity and expertise interweave in a dance of mutual respect and shared purpose. As the world grows more interconnected and complex, the art of collaboration becomes not just beneficial, but essential, catalyzing breakthroughs and enriching our collective understanding.

Google Docs

In the digital age, where real-time collaboration and accessibility are paramount, Google Docs stands as a pioneering force reshaping the landscape of document creation and editing. As a cornerstone of Google's suite of online productivity tools, it seamlessly blends the power of traditional word processing with the convenience of cloud-based technology. Users from across the globe can collaborate in real time, drafting, editing, and commenting simultaneously, transforming the solitary act of writing into a communal endeavor. With an intuitive interface and robust integration capabilities, Google Docs is more than just a tool—it's a testament to the possibilities of collaborative innovation in the modern era.

Dropbox Paper

In the evolving ecosystem of collaborative platforms, Dropbox Paper carves out its niche as a seamless fusion of simplicity and versatility. Birthed from the legacy of Dropbox—a titan in cloud storage—Paper elevates the collaborative experience by offering users a canvas where ideas, multimedia, and feedback coalesce in real-time harmony. Beyond mere text, its capabilities extend to dynamic content creation, from embedding videos to crafting to-do lists. As the boundaries of traditional document editing dissolve, Dropbox Paper emerges as a beacon of modern teamwork, where content creation and collaboration dance in synchronized rhythm.

Mind Mapping and Plotting

In the complex landscape of thought and creativity, mind mapping and plotting serve as guiding lights, illuminating pathways and connections that might otherwise remain obscured. These visual tools, harnessing the power of spatial organization, allow thinkers, writers, and planners to chart the terrain of their ideas, revealing both overarching themes and intricate details. Whether drafting the plot of a novel, strategizing a business venture, or conceptualizing a project, these diagrams act as living blueprints, evolving and adapting as thoughts mature and expand. As we navigate an increasingly complex world, the art of mind mapping and plotting becomes an essential compass, directing the journey from nascent idea to realized vision.

Scapple

Within the realm of tools designed for brainstorming and idea visualization, Scapple emerges as an intuitive canvas for free-form thought mapping. Crafted by the makers of the esteemed Scrivener, Scapple moves away from traditional rigid structures, granting users the freedom to draw connections, jot down ideas, and organize thoughts organically. It functions like a digital whiteboard, where the constraints of linear thinking are set aside in favor of a more fluid, associative approach. For writers, researchers, and creative minds seeking a space where ideas can dance freely and interconnect, Scapple offers a playground of boundless possibilities.

Plottr

In the artistry of storytelling, where narrative threads intertwine and characters come to life, Plottr emerges as a guiding compass for writers navigating the intricacies of their tales. This innovative software, specifically designed for plotting, provides a visual framework to map out storylines, character arcs, and key events in an interactive timeline. It's more than just a static outline; Plottr offers a dynamic canvas that adapts and evolves as the narrative takes shape. For both seasoned authors and budding storytellers, Plottr stands as a testament to the belief that every great story benefits from a well-laid plan.

Backup and Version Control

In the digital realm, where data reigns supreme and content undergoes perpetual evolution, the principles of backup and version control stand as twin pillars of security and organization. While backups ensure that our precious data remains shielded from unforeseen calamities, version control meticulously tracks each alteration, providing a chronological map of changes and iterations. These systems not only safeguard against loss but also empower creators and developers to revisit, compare, and refine their work with confidence. In an era defined by rapid technological advancements and constant content creation, mastering backup and version control becomes an indispensable skill, guarding the past while shaping the future.

Backupery for Scrivener

In the digital tapestry where meticulous writing meets the need for data protection, Backupery for Scrivener emerges as a tailored guardian. Recognizing the immense value and effort encapsulated within Scrivener projects, this tool offers scheduled backups, ensuring that every word, idea, and structure is preserved against potential technological mishaps. As writers pour their souls into intricate narratives and detailed research within Scrivener, Backupery stands vigilant, offering peace of mind with automated safety nets. It underscores a fundamental principle: while creativity may be boundless, it still deserves a secure harbor.

Git

In the intricate world of software development, Git stands as a linchpin of collaboration and version control. Conceived to manage and track modifications across vast codebases, Git has become an industry standard, allowing developers to merge their efforts, revert changes, and branch out with new features, all while maintaining the integrity of the project. But its influence extends beyond code; many professionals from varied fields now harness Git's powerful mechanisms to manage versions of their work. In this digital age, where precision and collaboration are paramount, Git serves as both a record keeper and a bridge, facilitating synergies and safeguarding progress.

Keep in mind that the best tool depends on your personal needs and workflow. While some writers might prefer comprehensive environments like Scrivener, others may favor a distraction-free space like OmmWriter. It's worthwhile to try out a few options to find what works best for you.

GLOSSARY

Adjectival modifier—An adjectival modifier can be a word, phrase, or clause that functions as an adjective to describe or clarify the meaning of a noun or pronoun. These modifiers provide additional information about the attributes, qualities, or characteristics of the noun or pronoun they modify. Examples include *your* country, a *turn-of-the-century style*, and *people who are always late*. These examples illustrate how adjectival modifiers enhance descriptions, allowing for more detailed and specific expressions in communication.

Adjective—Adjectives are words that modify nouns or pronouns by giving additional information about their quantity, quality, size, condition, or any other characteristic. They typically answer questions like "What kind?", "How many?", "Which one?", or "Whose?" For example, *awesome, best, both, happy, our, this, three, whose* and *yellow* are adjectives. Adjectives play a crucial role in adding detail and precision to sentences, enhancing both clarity and expressiveness in communication.

Adverb—Adverbs are words that modify or provide additional information about verbs, adjectives, other adverbs, or entire sentences, often indicating manner, frequency, degree, level of certainty, or timing. For example, *almost, also, eloquently, not, often, rapidly, really, someday, thus,* and *very* are adverbs. These examples illustrate the broad functional range of adverbs in enhancing the meanings and relationships between different parts of speech in sentences.

Adverbial phrase—An adverbial phrase is a group of words that functions as an adverb to modify a verb, an adjective, or another adverb by providing additional information about manner, time, place, frequency, or degree. For example, in the sentence *Landon laughs with abandon*, the phrase *with abandon* modifies the verb *laughs* to describe the manner of laughing. This example shows how adverbial phrases can enrich sentences by providing more detailed context to the actions or qualities they modify.

Agreement—Agreement refers to the correspondence of a verb with its subject in person and number (e.g., Lisa *goes* to Cal Tech; her sisters *go* to UCLA), and of a pronoun with its antecedent in person, number, and gender (e.g., As soon as Lisa finished the exam, *she* picked up *her* books and left the room).

Antecedent—An antecedent is a noun or noun phrase that a pronoun refers to or replaces later in the sentence or in subsequent sentences. It establishes the reference for the pronoun, allowing the sentence to maintain clarity and avoid repetition. For example, *Lexus* is the antecedent of *one* in the sentence: *I wanted a Lexus for my birthday but did not get one.* This is a classic usage of antecedents and pronouns to maintain coherence and conciseness in writing.

Apposition—Apposition refers to a grammatical construction in which two elements, usually noun phrases, are placed side by side, with one element serving to define or modify the other. Both elements must refer to the same thing or person. For instance, in *my friend Sue* and *the first U.S. president, George Washington*, "Sue" and "George Washington" respectively clarify "my friend" and "the first U.S. president." This construction is useful for providing additional information about a noun without creating a new sentence.

Appositive—An appositive is a noun or noun phrase that follows another noun immediately and explains or identifies it. It is usually set off by commas in the sentence. For example, His brother, *an accountant with Arthur Andersen* was recently promoted. Here, *an accountant with Arthur Andersen* is the appositive that provides additional information about "His brother" and is correctly punctuated with commas to indicate that it is an extra piece of information that renames or elaborates on the noun it follows.

Article—In English grammar, articles are considered a type of adjective because they modify nouns by specifying whether the nouns are specific or non-specific. Basically, an article is an adjective. Like adjectives, articles modify nouns. English has two articles: *the* and *a/an*. *The* is used to refer to specific or particular nouns; *a/an* is used to modify non-specific or non-particular nouns. We call the definite article *the*, and the indefinite article *a/an*.

Auxiliary verb—Auxiliary verbs, also known as "helping verbs," are used in conjunction with main verbs to express nuances of grammatical tense, aspect, mood, person, and voice. The most common auxiliaries are forms of *be*, *do*, and *have*. I *am* going; we *did* not go; they *have* gone. (See also *modal auxiliaries*.)

Case—The word case indicates how a noun or pronoun functions in a sentence. Personal pronouns have three cases: subject (for a subject or subject complement), object (for the object of a verb or preposition), and possessive. For example, for the pronoun *he*, *he* is the subject case, *him* is the object case, and *his* is the possessive case. Nouns and indefinite pronouns generally have two cases: the common case for both subject and object (e.g., *writer*, *someone*) and possessive (e.g., *writer's*, *someone's*).

Clause—A clause is a group of words that contains both a subject and a predicate. In English, there are two main types of clauses: independent and dependent.. For example, there are two clauses in the sentence, *although we looked for errors, we found none*. Note that *although we looked for errors* is a dependent clause (i.e., it cannot stand alone) and *we found none* is an independent clause (i.e., it can stand alone).

Collective noun—Collective nouns refer to groups as single entities, even though the group consists of multiple individuals or items. These nouns are singular in form and typically take a singular verb when the group is considered as a whole unit. Common collective nouns include *audience*, *government*, *herd*, and *public*.

Colloquialism—Colloquialisms are words or phrases that are used in informal speech or writing and are usually not suitable for formal contexts like academic or business communication. They often reflect regional dialects or everyday language and can make communication seem more casual or familiar. For example: They wanted to *get even* (instead of they wanted to *retaliate*).

Complement—Complements are words or phrases that complete the meaning of the predicate in a sentence. They are crucial for providing complete information about the subject or the object in a clause. There are two main types of complements: object complements and subject complements. *Object compliments* complete transitive verbs by describing or renaming the direct object: They found the play *exciting*. Ethan considers Jaimi *a wonderful wife*. *Subject complements* complete linking verbs and rename or describe the subject: Martha is my *neighbor*. She seems *shy*.

Compound adjective—Compound adjectives are formed by combining two or more words to create a single adjective that modifies a noun or pronoun. These adjectives often provide a specific, combined descriptor that enhances understanding or adds detail to the noun they modify. In English, compound adjectives are usually hyphenated when they precede the noun they modify to avoid ambiguity and ensure clarity (e.g., *bone-chilling*).

Compound noun—Compound nouns are formed by combining two or more words to create a new noun that represents a single concept. These nouns can appear in different forms. For example: *Hyphenated compound* connects the words with a hyphen (e.g., *free-for-all*). *Open compound* remains as separate words (e.g., *decision making*). *Solid compound* fuses the words together (e.g., *housekeeper*).

Compound sentence—A compound sentence consists of two or more independent clauses that are joined by a coordinating conjunction (such as *and, but, or, nor, for, so, yet*), a correlative conjunction (like *either... or, neither... nor*), or a semicolon. *Caesar conquered Gaul*, but *Alexander the Great conquered the world*, is a classic example of a compound sentence. It has two independent clauses: *Caesar conquered Gaul* and *Alexander the Great conquered the world*, which are joined by the coordinating conjunction *but*. This structure allows the sentence to express two related but distinct complete thoughts, providing a clear comparison between the two subjects.

Compound subject—A compound subject consists of two or more subjects combined by a conjunction to form a single, unified subject of the sentence (e.g., *Jack and Jill, either you or I*). If its parts are joined with *and*, the compound subject is usually plural, except when the parts form a single unit (e.g., *drinking and driving*) or refer to the same person or thing (e.g., *senior writer and editor*). If a compound subject contains *or* or *nor*, the verb agrees with the part nearest the verb.

Conjunction—Conjunctions are words that connect other words, phrases, or clauses within a sentence. They play a crucial role in building complex sentence structures and expressing various kinds of relationships between ideas. (See also *coordinating conjunctions, subordinating conjunctions,* and *correlative conjunctions.*)

Conjunctive adverb—Conjunctive adverbs are used to join two independent clauses together and to show the relationship between them, such as cause and effect, contrast, or sequence. These adverbs provide a smooth transition from one idea to another within a sentence or between sentences. Some of the most common conjunctive adverbs include *consequently, furthermore, hence, however, nevertheless, nonetheless* and, *therefore.* Conjunctive adverbs are not strong enough to join two independent clauses without the aid of a semicolon.

Contraction—Contractions are shortened forms of words or groups of words created by omitting certain letters and sounds, typically marked by an apostrophe in place of the omitted letters. Contractions are commonly used in spoken and informal written English to streamline communication and reflect natural speech patterns. For example: *can't* for cannot; *they're* for they are.

Coordinating conjunctions—Coordinating conjunctions are used to connect grammatical elements of equal rank, such as words, phrases, or independent clauses. For instance, connect elements of equal rank such as two nouns (e.g., *bread and butter*), two adjectives (e.g., *short and sweet*), two clauses (e.g., *the party was over, so they went home*). *And, but, or, nor, for, so* and *yet* are all the coordinating conjunctions.

Correlative conjunctions—Correlative conjunctions are pairs of words that work together to connect elements in a sentence, and they ensure balance and parallelism in the structure. They are used to link two equal grammatical items (e.g., *either . . . or, neither . . . nor,* and *not only . . . but also*).

Correlative expression—Correlative expressions, also known as correlative conjunctions, are pairs of words that work together to link and balance elements in a sentence. These expressions are a specific type of conjunction used to connect grammatically equivalent elements such as phrases or clauses. Common pairs include: *either . . . or, neither . . . nor,* and *not only . . . but also.* Using correlative expressions helps ensure parallel structure and clarity in sentence construction, emphasizing the relationship between the connected items.

Definite article—The definite article *the* is used in English to refer to specific nouns that are known to the reader or listener. It restricts the meaning of a noun to one particular thing or person (e.g., *the server crashed*) or person (e.g., *the* *minister spoke briefly*). The word *the* is the only definite article in the English language, and it can be used with both singular and plural nouns, as well as with both countable and uncountable nouns. This article helps to clarify that the noun it precedes is specific and definite, already familiar to the reader or listener or previously mentioned in the context.

Demonstrative pronoun—Demonstrative pronouns are used to point to specific things or people and are crucial in clarifying what is being referred to in a sentence. The primary demonstrative pronouns in English are *this*, *that*, *these*, and *those*. *This* and *these* refer to things that are nearby in space or time, while *that* and *those* refer to things that are farther away in space or further away in time.

Dependent clause—A dependent clause, also known as a subordinate clause, is a group of words that contains a subject and a verb but cannot stand alone as a complete sentence. In other words, it depends on an independent clause to form a complete thought. Dependent clauses begin with either a subordinating conjunction, such as *if, because, since*, or a relative pronoun, such as *who, which, that*. *When it gets dark*, we'll find a restaurant *that has music*.

Direct object—A direct object is a noun or noun phrase that receives the action of a transitive verb in a sentence. It directly experiences the action of the verb and answers the questions *what?* or *whom?* in relation to the verb. For example, the noun *report* is the direct object in the sentence *I handed in my monthly report*. It answers the question *I handed in what?*

Ellipsis (plural: ellipses)—Ellipsis can refer to two different concepts in writing: (1) As a grammatical term: Ellipsis is the omission of words that, while necessary for a grammatical structure, are not required to convey the intended meaning because they are implied by the context. For example, in the question and answer, *Who bought the cookies?* and *I did*, the phrase *buy the cookies* is understood and thus omitted. (2) As a punctuation mark: An ellipsis is a series of three dots (…) used to indicate the omission of words within a text, a pause in speech, trailing off of thought, or to build suspense. These dots can be spaced [. . .] as seen in formal writing, or unspaced […] as commonly used in informal texts. Both uses of an ellipsis serve to streamline communication by either omitting unnecessary details or indicating that something has been left unsaid.

Elliptical clause—This is a grammatically incomplete clause from which some words have been omitted, usually to avoid repetition. The meaning of an elliptical clause is typically clear from the context. For example, in the sentence *After reading that Jean has five dollars; Mary, three*, the words *has* and *dollars* are omitted in the second clause. This type of clause often uses a semicolon to separate it from a complete clause if directly related, and a comma to indicate the omission within the elliptical clause itself, helping maintain clarity and readability.

Gerund—A gerund is a verb form that ends in *-ing* and functions as a noun within a sentence. It can act as the subject, object, or complement in a sentence, essentially behaving like a noun while originating from a verb. For example, the gerund *smoking* acts as a noun in the sentence. *Smoking can be hazardous to your health*; the word *smoking* is a gerund acting as the subject of the sentence. It is derived from the verb *smoke*, but here it is used to name the action itself as a general concept or activity, which is then discussed as a subject of health concern. Gerunds are versatile and can be used in various grammatical roles, making them a useful tool for expressing activities or actions as nouns.

Indefinite article—An indefinite article is a type of article used before a noun to refer to a general, non-specific entity. In English, the indefinite articles are "a" and "an." "A" is used before words that begin with a consonant sound, and "an" is used before words that begin with a vowel sound. For example: *I saw a bird.* (Bird is any bird, not a specific one known to the speaker or listener.) *She ate an apple.* (Apple is any apple, not a specific one.)

Indefinite pronoun—Indefinite pronouns are used to refer to persons or things without specifying exactly who or what they are. They are called "indefinite" because they do not point to any specific person, thing, or amount in a definite manner. For example, indefinite pronouns convey ideas such as *all, another, any, anybody, anyone, anything, each, everybody, everyone, everything, few, many, nobody, none, one, several, some, somebody*, and *someone*.

Independent clause—An independent clause is a group of words that includes a subject and a verb and expresses a complete thought, allowing it to stand alone as a sentence. It doesn't need any additional information to be understood fully. For example: *Raccoons steal food.* It has a subject (*Raccoons*) and a verb (*steal*) and forms a complete thought, meaning it can stand alone as a sentence. Independent clauses are fundamental components of complex and compound sentences as well, where they may be joined with other independent or dependent clauses to elaborate on ideas or add depth to the narrative.

Indirect object—An indirect object identifies to whom or for whom the action of the verb is done. It typically comes between the verb and the direct object (though sometimes it may follow the direct object and be preceded by a preposition such as *to* or *for*). In the sentence *Don gave Betsy a set of fishing lures*, *Betsy* is the indirect object. It answers the question *to whom did Don give the fishing lures?*

Infinitive—An infinitive is a verb form that typically consists of the word *to* followed by the base form of a verb. This form is used in various ways within sentences, such as: *To write is to express oneself* (noun); *The decision to leave was difficult* (adjective); and *She came to help* (adverb). Infinitives are versatile and can express purposes, intentions, or potential actions, and they are not confined by subject or tense. They are a fundamental part of English grammar, helping to construct complex expressions and convey nuanced meanings.

Infinitive, split—A split infinitive occurs when an adverb or other word is inserted between "to" and the verb form in an infinitive. This can sometimes create emphasis or clarify the action being described. One of the most famous examples of a split infinitive is from the "Star Trek" introduction: *to boldly go where no man has gone before.* Here, *boldly* splits the infinitive *to go*, providing a dramatic effect and emphasizing the manner of going. While traditional grammar rules once frowned upon split infinitives, modern English usage accepts them, especially when they enhance clarity or the natural flow of a sentence. Split infinitives can make sentences sound more conversational and can be particularly useful in writing that seeks to engage or entertain.

Intensive pronoun—Intensive pronouns are used specifically for emphasis and are identical in form to reflexive pronouns. They refer back to another noun or pronoun in the sentence to emphasize it. Common examples include *myself, yourself, himself, herself, itself, ourselves, yourselves,* and *themselves.* For instance, in the sentence, *The president himself gave the order*, the intensive pronoun *himself* is used to emphasize that it was indeed the president and no one else who gave the order. This pronoun is not necessary for the grammatical structure of the sentence but is used to add emphasis to the subject. Intensive pronouns do not function as the object of a verb or preposition, unlike reflexive pronouns, which also reflect action back upon the subject but are essential to the sentence's meaning.

Interjection—Interjections are words or phrases that express strong emotion, surprise, or a sudden feeling and are typically separated from the rest of the sentence by punctuation such as a comma or an exclamation point. They can stand alone or be incorporated into larger sentences. The interjection, which is generally followed by an exclamation or a question mark, is often placed at the beginning or the end of a sentence. Some commonly used interjections are *Darn! Hey, you! Oops! Rats! Uh-uh!* and *Wow*! Interjections are versatile and can be placed at the beginning, middle, or end of sentences, depending on their usage and the desired impact on the reader or listener. They are particularly useful in dialogue or narrative writing to convey characters' emotions succinctly and vividly.

Interrogative pronoun—Interrogative pronouns are used specifically for asking questions. The main interrogative pronouns are *who, whom, which,* and *what*. Each serves a distinct function: *Who* is used to refer to people and acts as the subject of the question (e.g., *Who is coming to the party?*). *Whom* is also used to refer to people but acts as the object of the verb or preposition (e.g., *Whom did you invite?*). *Which* can refer to things or animals and is used when choosing among a set of known options (e.g., *Which book did you choose?*). *What* is generally used to refer to things and does not refer to known options as specifically as "which" does (e.g., *What happened here?*). These pronouns help construct clear and direct questions, each applying to different contexts and grammatical roles.

Intransitive verb—Intransitive verbs are verbs that do not require a direct object to complete their meaning. They express an action that does not pass from a doer to a receiver, and the action is contained within the subject. Examples of intransitive verbs include *growl* (e.g., *The bear is growling*), *crash* (e.g., *My computer crashed*), and *ring* (e.g., *The bell rang*). Each of these sentences makes complete sense without needing to add a direct object, demonstrating the intransitive nature of the verbs.

Linking verb—Linking verbs do not express action. Instead, they connect the subject of a sentence with a subject complement—a word or group of words that describes or identifies the subject. This complement can be a noun (nominative complement) or an adjective (predicate adjective). The verbs *be* (e.g., *My team leader is efficient*), *become* (e.g., *Julia became a doctor*) and *seem* (e.g., *The customer seems satisfied*) are all examples of linking verbs. Verbs of sensing (*look, feel, smell, sound, taste*) can also be used as linking verbs: e.g., *this stew smells good.*

Loose sentence—A loose sentence, also known as a cumulative sentence, starts with the main clause that expresses the central idea, and then adds on modifiers, qualifiers, and additional details. This structure places the important information at the beginning of the sentence, and the subsequent details provide elaboration or additional context. For example: *He was determined to succeed* (main idea) *with or without the promotion he was hoping for and in spite of the difficulties he was confronting at every turn* (additional details). This sentence structure is effective in English prose because it allows the reader to grasp the main point early on while the rest of the sentence enhances or elaborates on that point. It can also create a sense of spontaneity or conversational tone, reflecting the way thoughts often unfold in natural speech.

Main clause—A main clause, also known as an independent clause, is a clause that can stand alone as a grammatically complete sentence because it contains both a subject and a verb and expresses a complete thought. For example, *Grammarians quibble*, is an illustration of a main clause. It has a subject (*Grammarians*) and a verb (*quibble*) and forms a complete thought on its own.

Modal auxiliaries—Modal auxiliaries, also simply known as modals, are special verbs that modify the main verb in a sentence to express necessity, obligation, permission, probability, possibility, ability, or tentativeness. They do not change form according to the subject and are used alongside the base form of the main verb without "to". Here are examples of modal auxiliaries illustrating each use: necessity (*must*), obligation (*should*), permission (*may*), probability (*might*), possibility (*could*), ability (*can*), or tentativeness (*would*). Each modal provides a different nuance to the main verb, shaping the meaning of the sentence in terms of mood and modality.

Modifier—Modifiers are words, phrases, or clauses that provide additional information about other elements in a sentence. Their role is to qualify, describe, or limit the meaning of other words, typically nouns or verbs, making those words more specific or detailed. For example: *Frayed* ribbon, *dancing* flowers, *worldly* wisdom. Modifiers can enhance writing by adding color and detail to descriptions, thereby helping to paint a clearer picture or convey a specific tone. They can be essential for precision in language, providing clarity or emphasis to the nominal or verbal elements they accompany.

Nominative pronoun—Nominative pronouns are pronouns that function as the subject of a sentence or as a subject complement. These pronouns include: *I*, *we*, *you*, *he*, *she*, *it*, *they*, and *who*. They are used specifically in the nominative case, which means they are the ones doing the action or being described in the sentence.

For example: As subjects: *I* am going to the store, *We* watched a movie, *They* are on vacation. As subject complements: It is *I*, The winner is *she*, The one who called was *he*. These pronouns are essential for constructing clear and grammatically correct sentences in English, indicating who is performing the action of the verb or who is being described.

Non-restrictive modifier—A non-restrictive modifier, also known as a non-essential or non-defining modifier, is a phrase or clause that provides additional information about an element in a sentence but does not limit or define the essential meaning of that element. This additional information is not critical to understanding the main point of the sentence, and the sentence would still be clear and complete without it. For example: My youngest niece, *who lives in Ann Arbor*, is a magazine editor.

Noun—Nouns are words that name people, places, things, ideas, qualities, entities, or points in time. They serve as one of the fundamental elements of sentences, typically functioning as the subject or object within the sentence structure. For example, designates an idea (*immortality*), a person (*astronaut, Gretzky*), a place (*penalty box*), a thing (*canoe*), an entity (*Group of Seven*), a quality (*determination*) or a point in time (*tomorrow*).

Noun phrase—A noun phrase consists of a noun or pronoun and all the modifiers that describe or specify it. These modifiers can include articles, adjectives, and other nouns, as well as prepositional phrases and participle phrases that add further detail to the main noun. (e.g., *a shiny new Lexus, a glass of chocolate milk, the emergency room*). Noun phrases function as the subject, object, or complement in sentences, providing key information about what is being discussed or affected by the action of the verb.

Number—Number refers to the grammatical feature that denotes whether a noun, pronoun, or verb is singular or plural. This feature requires that words agree in number to ensure grammatical consistency within sentences. (1) Nouns and pronouns: These must match in number with other words they are connected with, especially verbs and antecedents. For instance, a singular noun requires a singular pronoun or verb, and a plural noun requires a plural pronoun or verb. (2) Verbs: These must agree with their subjects in number. A singular subject takes a singular verb, and a plural subject takes a plural verb. For example: A *solo flute plays* (*flute* is singular, so the verb *plays* is also singular). Two *oboes join* in (*oboes* is plural, so the verb *join* is also plural). This grammatical agreement ensures clarity and coherence in writing and speech, helping to maintain logical structure in communication.

Object—Object refers to a noun or pronoun involved in the action of a verb or located within a prepositional phrase. Objects can take several forms, depending on their function in the sentence: (1) Object of a preposition: This is the noun or pronoun that completes a prepositional phrase. For example, in *She sat on the chair*, "chair" is the object of the preposition "on." (2) Direct object: This is the noun or pronoun that receives the action of a transitive verb directly. It answers the question of *what? or whom?* relative to the verb. For example, in *She read the book*, "book" is the direct object of the verb "read." (3) Indirect object: This is the noun or pronoun that indirectly receives the action of the verb, usually appearing alongside a direct object. It answers the question of *to whom?* or *for whom?* the action is done. For example, in *She gave him a gift*, "him" is the indirect object, indicating the recipient of the gift. In the sentence *Frost offered his audience a poetic performance they would likely never forget*, "audience" is the indirect object, indicating to whom the performance was offered, and "a poetic performance" is the direct object, indicating what was offered.

Participial—A participial is a verb form that either collaborates with an auxiliary (helping) verb to form compound verb tenses or functions independently as an adjective. For example: As part of a compound tense: *They have been planning the event for months*. As an adjective: *Planning such an event requires dedication.* This definition clarifies the dual role of participles in English grammar, emphasizing their versatility in sentence construction.

Participial phrase—A participial phrase consists of a participle (either present or past) along with any accompanying modifiers, objects, or complements. These phrases function as adjectives, providing additional detail to nouns or pronouns in sentences. For example: The buzzards, *circling with sinister determination*, squawked loudly. Here, "circling with sinister determination" is the participial phrase. "Circling" is a present participle, and "with sinister determination" serves as a modifier that adds detail to how the buzzards are circling. The entire phrase modifies the noun "buzzards," providing more information about their action. Participial phrases enrich sentences by adding descriptive detail and can affect the pace and rhythm of writing, enhancing the overall narrative.

Participle—A participle is a form of a verb that functions as an adjective in a sentence. Participles come in two forms: *Present participle* ending in *-ing* (an in *a reading light*). *Past participle* often ends in *-ed* (as in *the produced goods*), but may be formed irregularly (as in *the eaten apple*). Participles are used to modify nouns and provide more detailed descriptions. They can stand alone or be part of a participial phrase that includes modifiers and complements.

Periodic sentence—A periodic sentence structures its main clause or key message at the end, creating suspense or emphasis by unfolding subordinate elements first. For example: *With or without their parents' consent, and whether or not they receive the assignment relocation they requested, they are determined to get married.* This format delays the resolution or main point until the conclusion, effectively engaging the reader's attention throughout the sentence.

Personal pronoun—Personal pronouns are used to refer to specific persons or things, and their forms change based on person, number, gender, and case. (1) *Subjective personal pronouns* are pronouns that act as the subject of a sentence, e.g., *I, you, she, he, it* and *they*. (2) *Objective personal pronouns* are pronouns that act as the object of the sentence, e.g., *me, you, her, him, it, us* and *them*. (3) *Possessive personal pronouns* are pronouns that show possession. They define a person (or a number or people) who owns a particular object, e.g., *mine, yours, hers, his, its, ours* and *theirs*.

Phrase—A phrase is a collection of related words that acts as a single unit within a sentence, but does not include both a subject and a verb. Phrases perform various grammatical functions, such as acting as nouns, verbs, adjectives, adverbs, or prepositions. Examples of phrases based on their functions include: *a quick decision* (noun phrase); *could have been running* (verb phrase); *extremely happy* (adjective phrase); *with great enthusiasm* (adverbial phrase); and *in the morning* (prepositional phrase). The example, *Without the resources to continue*, is a prepositional phrase that modifies a sentence by providing additional context about conditions or circumstances. This phrase, like others, lacks a complete subject and verb, making it an integral yet dependent part of the larger sentence structure.

Possessive—The possessive case in English grammar is used to denote ownership or possession, association, or other relationships between entities. This case applies to both nouns and pronouns, and it is marked in different ways: For nouns, possessiveness is typically indicated by adding an apostrophe and an "s" (e.g., *Harold's book*), or just an apostrophe for plural nouns that already end in "s" (e.g., *the dogs' bones*). For pronouns, possessive forms are unique words that do not require an apostrophe (e.g., *ours, mine, yours, his, hers, its, theirs*). These possessive forms help to clarify to whom or what something belongs, making sentences more precise and easier to understand.

Predicate—In a sentence, the predicate makes a statement about the subject and typically consists of a verb along with its objects, complements, and any modifiers related to these elements. The predicate tells what the subject does or what is done to the subject, including all pertinent details. For example, *handed in my application for the job* is the predicate of the sentence *I handed in my application for the job.* The predicate starts with the verb "handed in" and includes the direct object "my application" along with the prepositional phrase "for the job" which provides additional information about the action. This clear separation helps identify the action and details related to the subject of the sentence, which is "I" in this case.

Preposition—Prepositions are words that link nouns, pronouns, or phrases to other words within a sentence. They function to show the relationships between these elements, typically indicating location, direction, time, or a more abstract relationship. Common prepositions include *about, before, except, for, into, near, of, to, underneath* and *via*. A preposition may follow a verb to form a phrasal verb: e.g., *make use of (something), run into (someone)*. These examples, highlights another important function of prepositions in English grammar. In phrasal verbs, the preposition combines with a verb to create a new meaning, which is often idiomatic.

Prepositional phrase—A prepositional phrase is a group of words that includes a preposition, its object, and any modifiers of the object. These phrases provide additional information about location, time, direction, and other relationships within a sentence. For example, in *The keys are on the table*: *on* (preposition), *table* (object), and *the* "definite article (modifiers of the object). This structure helps clarify and detail the context of actions or the positioning of elements in a sentence.

Principal verb—The principal verb, also known as the main verb, is the central verb in a sentence that conveys the primary action or state of the subject in the main clause. For example, in *She runs every morning*, "runs" is the principal verb, indicating the main action performed by the subject. The principal verb can be accompanied by auxiliary verbs, which help express different tenses, moods, or voices, but the principal verb itself remains the focal point of the predicate. In *She* *has been running*, for instance, "running" is the principal verb, with "has been" serving as auxiliary verbs to detail the tense.

Pronominal—This term refers to anything related to or functioning as a pronoun. Pronominal elements include various forms of pronouns that serve different grammatical roles in sentences. Specifically, pronominal possessives, such as *hers*, *its*, and *theirs*, are types of pronouns that express ownership independently, without accompanying nouns. These pronouns are essential for referring back to previously mentioned nouns while avoiding repetition and providing clarity in communication.

Pronoun—Pronouns are words that substitute for nouns or noun phrases, helping to avoid repetitive use of nouns in speech and writing. They serve various functions and can represent people, objects, places, or ideas within a sentence. The words *I, you, it, me, them, mine, yours, herself, ourselves, someone, anything, few, each other, who* and *which* are all examples of pronouns.

Proper noun—Proper nouns refer to specific individuals, places, or things and are always capitalized to highlight their uniqueness. This distinguishes them from common nouns, which are more general and are not capitalized unless they begin a sentence or are part of a title. The name of a particular person (*Frank Sinatra*), place (*Boston*), or thing (*Moby Dick*). Proper nouns are capitalized. Common nouns name classes of people (*singers*), places (*cities*), or things (*books*) and are not capitalized.

Prose—Prose is a form of written or spoken language that mimics natural speech and follows standard grammatical structure, unlike structured poetry. It originates from the 14th century Old French term *prose*, derived from Latin *prosa oratio* meaning straightforward speech. While traditionally covering genres like philosophy, history, economics, journalism, and most fiction, prose contrasts with poetry, which often employs meter and rhyme. However, modern literary forms like free verse and prose poetry have blurred the distinctions between poetry and prose, as highlighted by T.S. Eliot's observation that the difference between poetry and prose is obscure.

Reflexive pronoun—Reflexive pronouns are used to refer back to the subject of the sentence or clause. They are essential when the subject and the object of the sentence are the same entity, or when the subject is performing an action upon itself. The reflexive pronouns used in writing are *myself, yourself, herself, himself,* *itself, ourselves, yourselves,* and *themselves.* These pronouns are vital for emphasizing that the action of the verb is directed back at the subject, and they help maintain clarity in sentence structure by indicating who is performing and receiving the action.

Relative clause—A relative clause is a type of dependent clause that modifies a noun or pronoun in the main clause. It is introduced by a relative pronoun, such as *who, which,* or *that,* or by a relative adverb, like *where, when,* or *why.* These clauses provide additional information or clarify details about the noun or pronoun they modify. For example: *The book that I borrowed was fascinating.* The relative clause "that I borrowed" provides more information about "the book." *We visited the house where I grew up.* The relative clause "where I grew up" adds details about "the house." Relative clauses enhance descriptions and add depth to narratives by integrating more detailed background information directly into sentences.

Relative pronoun—Relative pronouns are used to link clauses to their antecedents, thereby introducing relative clauses that provide additional information about the noun or pronoun referred to by the antecedent. For example, in the sentence: *The book that won the award is non-fiction,* the relative pronoun *that* introduces the relative clause *that won the award* and relates it to its antecedent *the book. That, which, who* and *whoever* are all relative pronouns.

Restrictive and nonrestrictive clauses—Restrictive clauses (also known as essential clauses) are integral to the meaning of the sentence because they define or limit the noun they modify. They are not set off by commas, as their information is crucial to understanding the full context of the sentence. (1) restrictive clause: Professional athletes *who perform exceptionally* should earn stratospheric salaries. Since there are no commas before and after the italicized clause, the italicized clause is restrictive and suggests that only those athletes who perform exceptionally are entitled to such salaries. (2) Conversely, nonrestrictive clauses (also known as non-essential clauses) provide additional information that can be helpful but is not critical to the fundamental meaning of the sentence. These clauses are typically set off by commas. If commas were added before *who* and after *exceptionally,* the clause would be nonrestrictive and would suggest that *all* professional athletes should receive stratospheric salaries—*Professional athletes, who perform exceptionally, should earn stratospheric salaries.*

Sentence fragment—A sentence fragment is a group of words that does not form a complete sentence because it lacks either a subject or a verb, or it does not express a complete thought, yet it is punctuated as if it were a complete sentence. For example: *Because it mattered greatly* is a fragment because it begins with a subordinating conjunction "because," making it dependent on additional information to form a complete sentence. It needs a main clause to be grammatically complete, such as in *She was upset because it mattered greatly*. Sentence fragments are often seen in informal writing or used stylistically in literature to convey a particular tone or effect, but in formal writing, they are usually avoided unless used deliberately for emphasis or a specific stylistic purpose.

Subject—The subject is typically a noun or pronoun that the sentence is about, and it's what the principal verb acts upon or describes. For example: *The new Steven Spielberg movie is a box office hit*. Here, "The new Steven Spielberg movie" is the subject of the sentence, and "is" is the principal verb that describes the state of the subject, indicating that it is a box office hit. This clear example demonstrates how the subject functions as the focus of the sentence, with the verb providing further information or action related to it.

Subordinate clause—A subordinate clause, also known as a dependent clause, does not express a complete thought and cannot stand alone as a sentence. It requires a main clause (independent clause) to form a complete sentence. For example: *After we finish our work*, we will go out for dinner. The subordinate clause "After we finish our work" provides additional information about the timing of the action described in the main clause. It is dependent on the main clause to form a full sentence with complete meaning.

Subordinating conjunctions—Subordinating conjunctions are words that begin a dependent (subordinate) clause and connect it to an independent (main) clause, establishing a relationship between the two. These conjunctions introduce clauses that provide necessary context such as time, reason, condition, contrast, and consequence to the main clause (e.g., *John woke the children after he ate breakfast*). Here, "after" is the subordinating conjunction that connects the dependent clause "he ate breakfast" to the main clause "John woke the children," specifying the sequence of events. Other common subordinating conjunctions include *although*, *because*, *if*, *when*, and *while*, each setting up different types of relationships (cause, time, condition, etc.) between the clauses they join. This structure is crucial for building complex sentences that convey detailed and nuanced information.

Syntax—Syntax refers to the rules and principles that govern the structure of sentences in a language, particularly the order and arrangement of words and phrases to create well-formed sentences. Syntax encompasses various techniques and structures, including parallelism and inversion, to convey meaning, emphasize certain elements, or achieve a specific rhetorical effect. For instance, syntax may exhibit parallelism (*I came, I saw, I conquered*), inversion (*Whose woods these are I think I know*), or other formal characteristics. These syntactic forms help shape how information is presented and understood, playing a critical role in communication effectiveness.

Tense—Tense in grammar refers to the form of a verb that indicates when an action or state of being occurs—past, present, or future. Tenses are critical in providing temporal context to the actions described in sentences. For example: the time of a verb's action or state of being, such as past, present, or future. *Saw, see, will see.* These verb forms help convey time frames and sequence events in narratives and descriptions, essential for clear communication about when things happen.

Transition—Transitions are words or phrases that help establish logical connections between sentences, paragraphs, or sections of text, aiding in the coherence and flow of writing. They guide the reader through the progression of ideas, showing relationships such as contrast, comparison, cause and effect, or sequence. For example *moreover* and *in addition*, are transitional words that effectively indicate a continuation or expansion of the thought process.

Transitive verb—Transitive verbs are verbs that require a direct object to complete their meaning, indicating what is receiving the action of the verb. Some transitive verbs can also take an indirect object, which indicates to whom or for whom the action is performed. For example, the verbs *find* (e.g., *You found your keys*), *glue* (e.g., *He glued the parts together*), and *put* (e.g., *I put the file on the desk*). These examples show how transitive verbs function within a sentence to connect the action of the verb to the object being acted upon, clearly demonstrating the dependency of these verbs on their objects for complete semantic meaning.

Verb—Verbs are essential parts of speech in any language, expressing actions, occurrences, or states of being. Verbs express an action (*break, call, tremble, skate*), an occurrence (*happen, occur*) or a state of being (*appear, become, seem*). Auxiliary (or helping) verbs are placed in front of a main verb to form a verb phrase. They have several functions; for example, they may help to create a different tense (e.g., *will* and *be* in the verb phrase *will be going*) or add an idea (e.g., the idea of obligation expressed by *must* in the verb phrase *must go*). These auxiliary verbs enhance the meanings of the main verbs and are integral in expressing detailed nuances in verb phrases.

Verb phrase—A verb phrase consists of a main verb along with any auxiliary (helping) verbs that accompany it. These phrases can convey nuanced meanings related to tense, mood, voice, or aspect. A verb phrase may also act as a predicate. For example, *can swim* is a verb phrase made up of the verb *swim* and its auxiliary *can* (indicating ability). This verb phrase also functions as the predicate in the sentence *John can swim*. Verb phrases are central to expressing complex actions and states in English, and they are crucial for constructing sentences that are grammatically complete and meaningfully detailed.

Verbal—Verbals are forms of verbs that function as nouns, adjectives, or adverbs in sentences, rather than acting as the main verb. There are three main types of verbals: (1) Gerunds: These are verb forms ending in -ing that function as nouns. For example, in *Swimming is enjoyable, swimming* is a gerund acting as the subject of the sentence. (2) Infinitives: These are the basic forms of verbs, usually preceded by "to." Infinitives can act as nouns, adjectives, or adverbs. For example, in *To read is to learn*, "to read" is an infinitive used as a subject. (3) Participles: These are verb forms used as adjectives. They can be present participles (ending in -ing) or past participles (often ending in -ed, -d, -t, -en, or -n). For example, in *The running water*, "running" is a present participle modifying "water." Verbals are versatile elements in English grammar that add richness and variety to sentence construction.

Voice—Voice refers to the form of a verb that indicates whether the subject of the sentence is performing the action (active voice) or receiving the action (passive voice). For example: Active voice: *Janet played the guitar*. Here, Janet is the subject performing the action of playing the guitar. Passive voice: *The guitar was played by Janet.* In this example, the guitar becomes the subject that is receiving the action, and Janet is introduced as the agent performing the action with the use of "by." Voice is a key aspect of verb conjugation in English and affects the clarity, conciseness, and dynamism of writing. Using active voice typically makes sentences more direct and vigorous, whereas passive voice can be useful for emphasizing the action itself or the recipient of the action rather than the doer.

BIBLIOGRAPHY

In many areas of publishing, it is difficult to fully understand the issues and the "rules of the road" without some background knowledge of basic writing, publishing, marketing, and selling your own books. Accordingly, due to the sheer volume of tasks involved, we have broken down the information into three chronological series: (1) AuthorsDoor Series: *Publisher & Her World*, (2) AuthorsDoor Advanced Series: *Publisher & Her World*, and (3) AuthorsDoor Masterclass Series: *Publisher & Her World*. The expansive curriculum, meticulously crafted, extends beyond texts—it includes books and workbooks. Recognizing the power of visual learning, we offer a series of free courses that illuminate the path for many on our Podcast and YouTube channels: Publisher and Her World at Ridge Publishing Group, AuthorsDoor Group, and Authors Red Door #Shorts.

AuthorsDoor Series: *Publisher & Her World*

The journey of a book from the seed of an idea to a place on a reader's shelf is filled with challenges, choices, and charm. In the vast literary universe, how does an author or publisher ensure their voice doesn't merely echo, but resonates? Enter the AuthorsDoor Series: *Publisher & Her World*, a meticulously crafted suite of books designed to illuminate every facet of the book industry.

In the AuthorsDoor Series: *Publisher & Her World*, we don't just discuss the art of writing; we delve into the experimentation of selling it. From the whispered secrets behind crafting engaging narratives and the magic of digital platforms to the meticulous science of metadata and the power of effective branding, each title in this series is a masterclass in itself:

1. **Secrets that Sell Books**: Delve into the art of messaging, unlocking techniques to influence audiences and revolutionize businesses.

2. **Websites that Sell Books**: Master the realm of digital real estate, ensuring your online presence is not just strong, but also strategic.

3. **Blog Sites that Sell Books**: Understand the bridge between casual conversations and committed readership.

4. **Social Media that Sells Books**: Navigate the vast social expanse, turning every post into a potential sale.

5. **Multimedia that Sells Books**: Step beyond traditional boundaries, embracing multimedia to captivate modern audiences.

6. **Metadata that Sells Books**: Dive into the behind-the-scenes magic that amplifies your book's digital footprint.

7. **Publishing that Sells Books**: Turn the intricate maze of publishing into a straight path toward success and recognition.

Whether you're an established author-publisher, a budding writer, or a curious reader eager to understand the mechanics behind your favorite titles, this series is your compass. The AuthorsDoor Leadership Program doesn't just open doors; it invites you into a world where every story is a potential bestseller.

Join me on a journey not just of discovery, but of mastery. Welcome to the AuthorsDoor Series: *Publisher & Her World.*

Secrets that Sell Books: Unlocking the Power of Messaging

The first book in the AuthorsDoor Series: *Publisher & Her World* is "Secrets that Sell Books: Unlocking the Power of Messaging." The book captivates readers, influences minds, and skyrockets your business success.

Summary:

In the vast ocean of published content, what makes one book rise above the rest? Dive into the transformative world of author branding, strategic copywriting, and savvy business planning. Whether you're a seasoned author or just embarking on your writing journey, this book offers a roadmap to ensure your books aren't just written, but are also read.

Part 1: The Book Called You – Understand that before selling a book, you're selling yourself. Hone your time management skills, establish a compelling author brand, and realize that your unique voice is its own market.

Part 2: The Rise of the Content Creators – Delve into the art and science of copywriting. Whether you write fiction or nonfiction, discover formulas that grip readers from the first word and keep them hooked until the last. Plus, master the timeless art of storytelling to elevate your business narrative.

Part 3: What Authors Need to Know – Ever thought about launching your own publishing house? Navigate the intricacies of author-publisher business structures, protect your intellectual property, and craft a business plan set for success. Unlock the power of strategic messaging and ensure your voice, and your books, rise above the noise.

Websites that Sell Books: Digital Dominance for Author-Publishers

The second book in the AuthorsDoor Series: *Publisher & Her World* is "Websites that Sell Books: Digital Dominance for Author-Publishers." Harness the web to amplify your brand, boost book sales, and elevate your business.

Summary:

In today's digital age, a website is more than just a digital storefront—it's your brand's heartbeat, the stage on which you perform, and the magnet that draws readers to your books. But how do you ensure that this essential tool isn't just aesthetically pleasing but also optimized to convert visitors into loyal readers?

Part 1: Author-Publisher Website Strategy – Your website is the cornerstone of your digital empire. Dive into the essentials: from establishing your unique author-publisher website and applying captivating design principles to mastering SEO techniques. Learn how to conduct a full site audit and ensure that your website remains a safe haven for your visitors.

Part 2: Content Management Tactics – Content is king, and your voice is its most powerful instrument. Discover the types of content your visitors are yearning for and refine your written voice for maximum impact. Delve into theme analysis to ensure your content remains cohesive, compelling, and search engine approved.

Part 3: Using Your Website Arsenal – With your website now primed, it's time to unleash its full potential. Boost your traffic through RSS feeds, syndication, backlinks, subscriptions, shareable content, and direct response paid advertising. Engage readers with compelling newsletters and, most crucially, discover strategies to monetize your site effectively.

Step into the digital realm with confidence, ensuring that every pixel of your website works diligently to elevate your brand, boost your sales, and amplify your success.

Blog Sites that Sell Books: Conversations that Convert

The third book in the AuthorsDoor Series: *Publisher & Her World* is "Blog Sites that Sell Books: Conversations that Convert." This volume focuses on author-publishers bridging the gap between blogs and book buyers.

Summary:

The modern author-publisher is no longer confined to the printed page. In the era of digital communication, the blog site becomes a dynamic stage—a place where authors can converse, captivate, and convert curious visitors into devoted readers. How can you, as an author-publisher, leverage this platform for maximum impact?

Part 1: Author-Publisher Blog Strategy – Delve deep into the foundation of a successful blog. Whether you're starting from scratch or refining an existing space, this section will guide you from conceptualizing your author-publisher blog to ensuring its security and continuous optimization. Grasp the intricacies of design and master the all-important realm of SEO.

Part 2: Content Management Tactics – Every word, image, and video on your blog tells a story. Learn to curate content that resonates, engages, and calls to action. Craft a comprehensive content marketing plan that encompasses the written word, compelling visuals, and engaging videos.

Part 3: Using Your Blog Site Arsenal – Your blog is armed and ready; now unleash its full power. Drive organic traffic through guest blogging, forge connections via backlinks, and turn your platform into a profit-generating machine. Embark on a journey from crafting conversations to bridging the gap between your blog and book buyers. Turn every post into an opportunity and every visitor into a fan.

Social Media that Sells Books: From Posts to Profits

The fourth book in the AuthorsDoor Series: *Publisher & Her World* is "Social Media that Sells Books: From Posts to Profits." This book provides a social media blueprint that engages readers and drives sales.

Summary:

In the bustling digital marketplace, the line between a casual browser and a dedicated reader is often a well-crafted social media post. But how does one convert casual likes into loyal book purchases? Navigate the intricate maze of social media with a blueprint designed to both engage readers and convert them into sales.

Part 1: Social Authority Marketing Strategy – Building a robust online presence is more than just frequent posting; it involves crafting a strategic approach. Learn how to hone your voice, tailor your message to the right audience, and harness the power of social testing to discover what truly resonates.

Part 2: A Handful of Social Media Marketing Tactics – With a plethora of platforms at your disposal, knowing where and how to market is crucial. Dive deep into tailored campaigns for LinkedIn, Facebook, Instagram, Twitter, and Pinterest. Each platform offers unique avenues to reach potential readers, and this section equips you to capitalize on each one.

Part 3: Using Your Social Media Arsenal – Now armed with knowledge and tactics, it's time to engage! Drive traffic to your platforms, participate in thriving communities, and harness the power of hashtags. And when you're ready, unlock strategies to efficiently monetize your networks efficiently through paid media.

Step into the world of social media with clarity and confidence, and turn every interaction into a potential sale.

Multimedia that Sells Books: Beyond Text

The fifth book in the AuthorsDoor Series: *Publisher & Her World* is "Multimedia that Sells Books: Beyond Text." This book offers a multimedia strategy that engages, enthralls, and converts readers.

Summary:

In an age where attention spans are fleeting, how do author-publishers captivate and hold the interest of readers? The answer lies in transcending traditional boundaries and embracing the immersive power of multimedia. Dive into a comprehensive book that reveals how to harness visuals, audio, and entertainment to elevate your books' appeal.

Part 1: A Visual World – They say a picture is worth a thousand words. Delve into the captivating realms of photography, animation, and cutting-edge art technologies. Learn the nuances of editing, the dynamism of GIFs, and the wonders of CGI and AI in visual storytelling.

Part 2: A Hearing World – Sound is emotion personified. Whether it's the cadence of an author's voice or the ambient noise that sets a scene, discover how to create and edit audio that resonates. Plus, master the art of podcast marketing to reach a wider, auditory-focused audience.

Part 3: An Entertainment World – Video isn't just a medium; it's an experience. Understand the intricacies of video editing, launch impactful YouTube campaigns, and explore the cinematic potential of film in the context of book marketing.

Step beyond the written word. Immerse your audience in multimedia symphony that not only engages and enthralls but also persuasively converts.

Metadata that Sells Books: Mastering the Digital Pulse

The sixth book in the AuthorsDoor Series: *Publisher & Her World* is "Metadata that Sells Books: Mastering the Digital Pulse." Harness metadata to elevate your story and monetize your craft.

Summary:

Behind every successful book in the digital realm lie an unseen force: metadata. But how do authors harness this behind-the-scenes powerhouse to make their works shine brighter and sell better? Dive into the intricate world of metadata and uncover the strategies that can elevate your narrative and boost your book's profitability.

Part 1: The Book Package – Begin by laying a robust foundation. From strategic book planning to optimizing your Amazon product page, discover how Amazon's publishing imprints can be your book's best allies.

Part 2: Sales Funnel Channel – The perfect title, a captivating cover, an irresistible blurb. Each element of your book plays a pivotal role in enticing potential readers. Explore how to optimize these touchpoints, understand the power of Amazon's "Look Inside" feature, and recognize the profound impact of authentic reviews.

Part 3: Amazon Publishing Tools – Amazon isn't just a sales platform; it's a treasure trove of tools waiting to be harnessed. Perfect your Amazon Author Profile, leverage Kindle programs to your advantage, and navigate the collaborative realm of Goodreads for book discovery.

In the modern publishing landscape, mastering metadata isn't just an option—it's essential. Equip yourself with the knowledge to navigate the digital pulse, ensuring your story reaches its deserved audience and your craft yields its true potential.

Publishing that Sells Books: Master the Publishing Maze

The seventh book in the AuthorsDoor Series: *Publisher & Her World* is "Publishing that Sells Books: Master the Publishing Maze." Navigate top platforms to boost exposure and drive sales.

Summary:

In a world overflowing with stories, how does an author ensure their voice is heard and their work is seen? The answer lies not just in crafting a compelling narrative, but in navigating the intricate maze of publishing with skill and finesse. Delve into a comprehensive book designed to illuminate every twist and turn of the publishing journey.

Part 1: Pre-Production Works – Before your book meets its readers, it undergoes a transformation. Discover the nuances of formatting for e-books, print, and audio. Perfect the art of creating files that are tailored for electronic and print platforms, ensuring your book's presentation matches its content's brilliance.

Part 2: Amazon and IngramSpark: Best of Both Worlds – Two giants. Multiple opportunities. Explore the vast ecosystems of Amazon and IngramSpark. Whether it's e-books, print, or audio, understand the intricacies of each platform and how to make them work in harmony for your book's success.

Part 3: Upload Your Book to e-Resellers – Widen your horizons and reach audiences across varied platforms. Dive into the specifics of platforms like Nook

Press, Draft2Digital, Smashwords, iTunes, Kobo Writing Life, and Google Play Books, turning each into a conduit for your story.

Embark on your publishing journey with confidence. With the right map in hand, turn the complex maze of publishing into a straight path towards success, exposure, and unparalleled sales.

AuthorsDoor Advanced Series: *Publisher & Her World*

The world of authorship is ever-evolving, and for every word penned, there is a strategy to market it, a campaign to advertise it, a brand to encapsulate it, and a platform to publicize it. The AuthorsDoor Advanced Series: *Publisher & Her World* is an odyssey into the more intricate and nuanced layers of the literary universe, where writing meets the advanced facets of commerce and recognition.

This series ventures beyond the basics, exploring the deeper currents that shape a book's journey from manuscript to marketplace:

1. **Writing that Sells Books**: Unearth the nuances of crafting narratives that don't just tell stories, but also ensure they are bought and read.

2. **Marketing that Sells Books**: Delve into innovative strategies that elevate books from mere listings to must-haves.

3. **Advertising that Sells Books**: Navigate the dynamic world of advertising, understanding how to capture attention in an age of information overload.

4. **Branding that Sells Books**: Explore the essence of a book, an author, and a publisher, and learn how to convey that essence to readers in an unforgettable way.

5. **Publicity that Sells Books**: Harness the power of the media, both online and offline, turning every mention into a potential sale.

The AuthorsDoor Advanced Series is for those who aren't just content with writing a book, but are passionate about ensuring their work reverberates in the hearts and minds of readers everywhere. It's for those who see the bigger picture, where art meets strategy, and where stories meet success.

Step into a realm where writing is just the beginning, and where every page turned reveals deeper insights and strategies. Welcome, once again, to *Publisher & Her World*, this time with advanced tools at your disposal.

Writing that Sells Books: Pen to Profit

The first book in the AuthorsDoor Advanced Series: *Publisher & Her World* is "Writing that Sells Books: Pen to Profit." Cultivate the author-publisher mindset for financial freedom.

Summary:

Transform your passion for writing into a thriving enterprise. From the spark of an idea to managing a full-fledged publishing house, this book reveals the intricacies of the author-publisher journey, unlocking the gates to financial freedom. Dive into an invaluable resource that melds the artistic spirit with business acumen.

Part 1: Millionaire Writing Mindset – Kickstart your journey with answers to pressing questions. Envision and establish your publishing entity, pinpoint your genre positioning, conduct deep consumer market research, and equip yourself with a plethora of innovative marketing and sales strategies.

Part 2: Writing and Editing Bestselling Titles – The heart of every publishing endeavor: the manuscript. Whether you're a solo writer, collaborating with others, or employing ghostwriters, ensure your work shines with clarity and precision through expert development and meticulous editing.

Part 3: Self-Publishing a Successful Book – Venture into the nuts and bolts of bringing your work to life. Immerse yourself in the art of book design, understand pre-press production, navigate the world of book manufacturing, and uncover the magic behind bookbinding.

Part 4: Running a Full Service Publishing House – For those with an expansive vision, master the operational side of the publishing world. Delve into distribution, warehousing, and fulfillment strategies. Learn to manage the business side efficiently and consider avenues for growth and expansion.

Embark on a journey from penning words to reaping profits. Nurture the mindset, harness the skills, and unlock the strategies that pave the way to a flourishing author-publisher career.

Marketing that Sells Books: Digital Mastery for Book Sales

The second book in the AuthorsDoor Advanced Series: *Publisher & Her World* is "Marketing that Sells Books: Digital Mastery for Book Sales." This guide explores leveraging blogs, social media, videos, and viral tactics to engage and convert readers.

Summary:

In the vast digital arena, every author seeks the spotlight. But how does one rise above the noise, capturing attention and converting it into sales? Dive deep into a comprehensive book that marries traditional and digital marketing, offering a toolkit to engage readers like never before.

Part 1: Millionaire Marketing Mindset – Begin with reshaping your perspective. Address your burning questions, adopt the mindset of a market leader, and craft a robust marketing plan. With a strategic roadmap tailored for both offline and online spaces, and a wealth of innovative marketing and selling ideas, lay the foundation for unparalleled success.

Part 2: Marketing Books that Sell – Extend your reach beyond conventional book marketing. Harness the power of email campaigns, newsletters, and the untapped potential of magazine and e-zine marketing to create ripples in the market.

Part 3: Offline Marketing Strategy – Explore the tangible realm of marketing. Dive into the world of book clubs, allure readers with enticing merchandise, and embark on effective indie-bound marketing campaigns that cement your presence in physical spaces.

Part 4: Online Store Marketing Tactics – Turn the virtual marketplace into your playground. Whether it's the vast expanse of Amazon, the social hubs of Facebook, Instagram, and Pinterest, or niche spaces like Etsy and eBay, master the art of selling where the readers are.

Step into the dynamic world of book marketing with confidence. Equip yourself with strategies, insights, and tools that promise not just visibility but also impactful engagement and impressive sales.

Advertising that Sells Books: Web-Ad Wizardry

The third book in the AuthorsDoor Advanced Series: *Publisher & Her World* is "Advertising that Sells Books: Web-Ad Wizardry." Craft copy that captures readers and seals the sale

Summary:

Navigate the world of advertising as if you held the map. Dive into a comprehensive book that demystifies the advertising landscape, offering both novice and seasoned authors the keys to captivating readers and sealing those crucial sales.

Part 1: Millionaire Advertising Mindset – Advertising begins in the mind. Address all your pressing questions, embrace the mindset of a sales leader, and craft a robust advertising plan. With strategic roadmaps and a treasure trove of inventive advertising and selling concepts, set the stage for an impactful campaign.

Part 2: Advertising Books that Sell – Words wield power. Master the art of copywriting, understand the nuances of compelling advertising, and explore the lucrative avenue of selling advertising space in a business-to-business (B2B) setting.

Part 3: Offline Advertising Strategy – Explore the art of offline advertising, where creativity meets precision. Delve into the miracles of market research to tailor your campaigns to the ideal audience. Understand the impact of artistic elements in advertising and how they capture attention and communicate messages effectively. Additionally, master the tactics of direct mail advertising to reach your audience directly in their homes, creating a personal and persuasive appeal that drives reader engagement and sales.

Part 4: Online Advertising Tactics – The digital domain offers a multitude of channels, each with its unique charm. Whether it's the visibility of banner ads, the precision of pay-per-click (PPC), or the expansive reach of Google's offerings, become adept at utilizing each tool. Plus, understand affiliate programs and guard against the pitfalls of PPC fraud.

Step into the realm of advertising armed with knowledge, insights, and strategies. With every ad, capture the imagination of readers, and with every sale, inch closer to your authorial dreams.

Branding that Sells Books: Brand Brilliance

The fourth book in the AuthorsDoor Advanced Series: *Publisher & Her World* is "Branding that Sells Books: Brand Brilliance." Harness your company's crown jewel to fuel profitable growth.

Summary:

In a saturated market, a strong brand isn't just a luxury—it's a necessity. Step into a masterclass that reveals how the pseudoscience of branding can transform your offerings from mere products to must-haves. Discover how to turn your brand, whether it's your company, your author persona, or your individual books, into a beacon for readers everywhere.

Part 1: Millionaire Branding Mindset – Every great brand begins with a vision. Start your journey by addressing foundational questions, adopt the mindset of a brand trailblazer, and designing a brand plan that's both visionary and actionable. With strategic insights and a multitude of innovative branding and selling ideas, set the tone for a brand that resonates.

Part 2: Brand Story – Your brand tells a story. Delve deep into the nuances of crafting compelling narratives across different facets, be it as a publisher, an author, or for specific products. Understand that each element is a chapter in the grand tale you wish to tell.

Part 3: Offline Branding Strategy – The physical world offers a canvas rife with opportunities. From promotional endeavors to leveraging print media, learn how to make an indelible mark. Additionally, master the craft of penning opinions and articles that not only enhance your brand but also position you as a thought leader in online publications.

Part 4: Online Branding Tactics – The digital domain is where brands come alive. Understand the art and science of brand discovery, leverage the power of social bookmarking, and stay attuned to the pulse of your brand with advanced monitoring tools like Google Alerts and Mention.

Embark on a journey to brand mastery. With the right tools and strategies, craft a brand that doesn't just capture attention, but also hearts, ensuring sustained growth and profitability.

Publicity that Sells Books: Powerful PR on a Budget

The fifth book in the AuthorsDoor Advanced Series: *Publisher & Her World* is "Publicity that Sells Books: Powerful PR on a Budget." Craft impactful publicity campaigns without breaking the bank.

Summary:

The art of publicity is not in lavish campaigns, but in crafting narratives that resonate and linger. Dive into an insightful book that unveils how to mount impactful publicity campaigns without stretching your finances. Whether you're an established author or a budding writer, this book is your roadmap to making waves in the world of public relations (PR).

Part 1: Millionaire Publicity Mindset – Begin by tuning your mind. Address those burning questions, embrace the mindset of a pioneering publicist, and craft a robust public relations plan. Equipped with strategic directives and a plethora of inventive PR and selling concepts, lay the foundation for campaigns that captivate.

Part 2: Brand Influencer – The digital age has rewritten the rules of PR. Understand this transformation, appreciate PR's pivotal role in branding, and master the art of writing materials that don't just inform but also influence.

Part 3: Offline PR Strategy – The tangible world offers its unique charm. From orchestrating grand publicity campaigns and securing coveted media exposure to harnessing the power of book directories, navigate the multifaceted avenues of offline PR.

Part 4: Online PR Tactics – The online realm is a playground of possibilities. Discover how to leverage PR in our interconnected, social world. Delve deep into the nuances of wired PR and establish a commanding presence with a dynamic online media room.

Step into the spotlight with confidence. With this book by your side, craft campaigns that don't just generate buzz but also build enduring relationships, ensuring your books fly off the shelves.

AuthorsDoor Masterclass Series: *Publisher & Her World*

Every masterpiece is built on a foundation of intricacies, details that might escape the casual observer but are instrumental to the artisan. In the vast expanse of literary craftsmanship, these intricacies determine the difference between a good book and a magnum opus. The AuthorsDoor Masterclass Series: *Publisher & Her World* offers a dive into these critical facets, providing a meticulous exploration of topics that every author-publisher must master.

While the previous series guided you through the broader landscapes of the literary world, this series zooms in, shedding light on the granular elements that, though sometimes overlooked, are pivotal to success:

1. **AuthorsDoor Leadership Program for Business Owners**: Unleash your executive potential: Transform your approach and lead your business to unparalleled success.

2. **Personal Branding and Influence**: Master the art of personal branding and influence to navigate and excel in the digital age, transforming your online and offline presence into a powerful, persuasive force.

3. **Time Management**: Unlock the secrets to bending time in your favor with proven strategies that empower you to achieve more, stress less, and take control of your daily life.

4. **Power Posting**: Master the art of impactful social media with practical, powerful strategies to make your presence pop in a crowded digital landscape.

5. **The Author-Publisher's Playbook**: Unlock the secrets to becoming a bestseller with 1000+ innovative and proven tactics designed to market and sell your book like a publishing pro.

The AuthorsDoor Masterclass Series is more than just a guide—it's an invitation to the sanctum sanctorum of the publishing world. It's for those who understand that mastery lies in the details and who aren't satisfied with just knowing the *what* and the *how* but are hungry for the *why*.

Embark on this final leg of your educational journey with the AuthorsDoor Leadership Program, refining your craft, sharpening your knowledge, and preparing not just to participate in the literary world, but to lead. Welcome to the AuthorsDoor Masterclass Series: *Publisher & Her World*, inner circle.

AuthorsDoor Leadership Program for Business Owners: Driving Success at the Highest Levels

The first book in the AuthorsDoor Masterclass Series: *Publisher & Her World* is "AuthorsDoor Leadership Program for Business Owners: Driving Success at the Highest Levels."

Summary:

Welcome to the "AuthorsDoor Leadership Program for Business Owners," a masterclass designed to elevate your leadership to the highest levels of success. This book delves into the crucial elements that shape successful business leaders across various sectors, including the role of author-publishers.

Part 1: Millionaire Business Mindset – Explores foundational leadership strategies, such as business planning and marketing tactics, to refine your approach to business leadership and market engagement.

Part 2: Fundamentals of C-Level Leadership – Offers insights into key executive roles, detailing the responsibilities and strategic importance of each position to enhance corporate synergy and effectiveness, applicable whether you're a sole-proprietor or head of a larger enterprise.

Part 3: Strategic Vision and Decision Making – Focuses on developing strategic vision and decision-making skills, with an emphasis on innovation, team building, effective communication, and crisis management to strengthen leadership capabilities.

Part 4: Cultivating Core Leadership Qualities – Highlights personal development strategies to enhance executive presence and influence, aiming to transform leaders into influential figures who inspire and lead with confidence and foresight.

This comprehensive book guides you on a transformative journey through the nuanced layers of leadership and management. Each part builds upon the last, equipping business owners with the tools necessary for effective and influential leadership. The AuthorsDoor Masterclass Series: *Publisher & Her World* not only deepens your understanding of operational mechanics and strategic planning but also emphasizes personal growth and impact. As you progress through each book within the series, you'll be prepared not just to manage your businesses but to redefine your industry and lead with unparalleled success and vision.

Personal Branding and Influence:
Crafting a Compelling Personal Brand in a Connected World

The second book in the AuthorsDoor Masterclass Series: *Publisher & Her World* is "Personal Branding and Influence: Crafting a Compelling Personal Brand in a Connected World."

Summary:

"Personal Branding and Influence" serves as an indispensable guide for professionals, entrepreneurs, and creatives who aim to establish a distinctive personal brand in today's multifaceted digital and physical environments. This book lays out a strategic roadmap for navigating the complexities of personal branding, starting with the foundational elements of identifying personal values, professional objectives, and unique strengths.

Part 1: Foundations of Personal Branding – This section delves into the basics of building a personal brand, from defining personal branding itself to crafting your personal narrative.

Part 2: Developing Your Brand Message and Audience – It guides you through the process of identifying your core message, understanding your target audience, and effectively using digital tools to communicate your brand

Part 3: Amplifying Your Brand – Offers advanced strategies for enhancing your visibility and influence through social media, podcasting, blogging, and other digital mediums.

Part 4: Sustaining and Evolving Your Brand – Tackles the ongoing challenges of maintaining digital etiquette, adapting to changes, and ensuring authenticity and consistency in your branding efforts.

This comprehensive guide not only teaches you how to create and amplify a powerful personal brand but also how to sustain and evolve this brand over time. It equips you with the tools necessary to become a persuasive communicator and respected leader, enhancing both your professional and personal life. Whether you are launching a new venture, seeking to advance your career, or aiming to revamp your professional image, this book offers invaluable insights and practical advice to achieve success and make a lasting impact.

Time Management: Mastering the Clock Before It Masters You

The third book in the AuthorsDoor Masterclass Series: *Publisher & Her World* is "Time Management: Mastering the Clock Before It Masters You."

Summary:

"Time Management: Mastering the Clock Before It Masters You" is a vital guide for authors, publishers, marketers, and publishing executives seeking to master their schedules and boost productivity in the fast-paced literary and publishing sectors. This book offers practical, actionable strategies tailored to the unique demands of the industry, beginning with a deep dive into the psychology of time management and the common pitfalls of procrastination and mismanagement.

Part 1: Understanding Time Management Challenges – Introduces the foundational concepts of time management within the publishing industry, exploring psychological barriers and assessing current time usage to set the stage for improvement.

Part 2: Core Time Management Strategies – Outlines specific techniques such as Manuscript Time Blocking, Publication Priority Coding, and Social Media Efficiency Strategies, aimed at maximizing productivity across writing, marketing, and administrative tasks.

Part 3: Advanced Application and Tools – Delves into the use of digital tools to enhance productivity, project management techniques, and strategies for building an efficient team, providing readers with the skills to implement these systems in their daily routines.

Part 4: Long-Term Sustainment and Case Studies – Focuses on sustaining improvements over time, creating a culture of productivity, and includes case studies showcasing successful time management practices in action.

This comprehensive guide not only equips publishing professionals with the tools to better manage their time but also emphasizes the development of strategies to maintain these practices long-term. The insights and techniques provided will help readers navigate their busy schedules more effectively, allowing them to focus on what truly matters—creating and selling great content.

Power Posting: Crafting a Social Presence that Stands Out

The fourth book in the AuthorsDoor Masterclass Series: *Publisher & Her World* is "Power Posting: Crafting a Social Presence that Stands Out."

Summary:

"Power Posting" is an indispensable guide for individuals and businesses looking to significantly enhance their impact on social media. This book dives deep into strategic and practical techniques designed to elevate your social media presence and engage effectively in the increasingly competitive digital space.

Part 1: Building the Foundation – Focuses on the essentials of using social media as a branding tool. It covers analyzing your current presence, setting strategic objectives, understanding your audience, and crafting a comprehensive social media strategy.

Part 2: The Art of Content Creation – Delve into the elements of creating engaging content. Learn to craft powerful headlines, master visual storytelling, and optimize posting times across various platforms.

Part 3: Engagement and Community Building – Explores how to leverage trends and foster meaningful interactions to build a dedicated community. This section emphasizes the use of analytics to refine strategies and the benefits of effective influencer collaborations.

Part 4: Advanced Tactics and Crisis Management – Provides insights into sophisticated strategies for boosting engagement and managing social media crises. It ensures a strong, positive online brand presence and offers advice on maintaining a consistent brand voice and planning for long-term success.

Equipped with actionable advice, real-world examples, and expert tips, "Power Posting" is an essential resource for marketers, small business owners, and influencers. It ensures that every post counts, contributing distinctly to a unique and influential social media presence that resonates with your audience and fosters lasting engagement. Unlock the full potential of your social media with this comprehensive guide.

The Author-Publisher's Playbook:
1000+ Tactics to Market and Sell Your Masterpiece

The fifth book in the AuthorsDoor Masterclass Series: *Publisher & Her World* is "The Author-Publisher's Playbook: 1000+ Tactics to Market and Sell Your Masterpiece."

Summary:

"The Author-Publisher's Playbook" is the ultimate guide for author-publishers poised to conquer the competitive publishing market. This manual unveils over 1000 tried-and-tested tactics, offering a detailed, strategic approach to the entire publication process—from understanding the market to sustaining success post-launch.

Part 1: Market Analysis and Brand Development – Introduces readers to the publishing landscape, helping them identify their niche, develop a strong author brand, and optimize their online presence to effectively attract and engage potential readers.

Part 2: Strategic Marketing and Engagement – Delves into a vast array of marketing strategies, covering effective email campaigns, media partnerships, social media prowess, and content marketing tactics designed to boost engagement and visibility.

Part 3: Sales Optimization and Distribution Channels – Discusses optimal distribution strategies, online sales maximization, and innovative advertising techniques to ensure extensive reach and reader engagement.

Part 4: Sustaining Success Post-Launch – Offers strategies for maintaining momentum after the book launch, including garnering reviews, capitalizing on awards, and developing a long-term brand strategy to keep sales consistent and profile elevated.

"The Author-Publisher's Playbook" is more than a mere collection of strategies; it's a robust toolkit designed to prepare author-publishers for every aspect of the book marketing and sales journey. Packed with actionable advice, real-world examples, and expert tips, this playbook is essential for anyone starting out or seeking to enhance their existing strategies, ensuring they are well-equipped to turn their publishing endeavors into profitable ventures.

Empire Builders Series:
Masterclasses in Business and Law

In the dynamic world of business, where innovation intersects with opportunity, success often hinges not only on creativity but also on a deep understanding of the legal and operational landscapes. The Empire Builders Series is meticulously designed to arm aspiring entrepreneurs, seasoned business owners, creative professionals, and legal experts with the comprehensive knowledge and strategies needed to navigate these complexities and build lasting empires.

Each book in the series serves as a foundational pillar, offering expert guidance and actionable insights in specific areas of business and law; tailored to foster growth, innovation, and success in today's competitive marketplace:

1. **Brick by Brick**: This guide acts as your blueprint for building a business from the ground up. It offers essential strategies, legal insights, and operational tactics crucial for establishing a solid foundation for any business venture.

2. **Mark Your Territory**: Dive deep into the world of trademarks with this essential guide, designed to help you protect and effectively leverage your brand in today's competitive market.

3. **From Idea to Empire**: Transform your entrepreneurial dreams into reality with this exhaustive guide to business planning. Learn how to craft a compelling business plan that not only attracts investors but also sets the stage for a successful enterprise.

4. **Beyond the Pen**: Safeguard your creative works and master the intricacies of copyright law with this expert guide, tailored specifically for writers, artists, musicians, and digital content creators.

5. **Legal Ink**: Demystify the complex legal landscape of publishing with practical advice on negotiating contracts and protecting intellectual property, essential for authors and publishers.

The Empire Builders Series stands as a testament to the power of knowledge and the importance of mastering the strategic and legal aspects of business management. Each book is designed not merely to inform but to inspire action and lead to success. Embark on this journey to build your empire, one masterclass at a time.

Brick by Brick: The Entrepreneur's Guide to Constructing a Company

The first book in the Empire Builders Series: Masterclass in Business and Law is "Brick by Brick: The Entrepreneur's Guide to Constructing a Company."

Summary:

"Brick by Brick" is an indispensable resource for entrepreneurs who are poised to transform their innovative business ideas into successful enterprises. This comprehensive guide meticulously outlines the complexities of business formation, providing detailed, step-by-step instructions and vital insights into the legal, operational, and strategic aspects of starting and running a thriving company.

Part 1: Laying the Foundation – Focuses on selecting the appropriate business entity, delving into the legal implications of each option and the economic considerations vital for establishing a solid foundation for your business.

Part 2: Operational Mechanics – Discusses the operational aspects of setting up partnerships and LLCs, navigating corporate governance, maintaining corporate records, and managing capital and shareholder relationships effectively.

Part 3: Advanced Strategic Planning – Offers insights into managing structural changes, handling stock and ownership issues, expanding operations across state lines, and deploying tax strategies to ensure compliance and optimize financial performance.

Part 4: Implementation Tools and Resources – Provides practical tools such as sample agreements, startup task checklists, and comprehensive guidelines for drafting business plans and the incorporation process, enabling entrepreneurs to effectively implement their business strategies.

"Brick by Brick" not only serves as a guide but acts as a complete blueprint for building a robust business capable of thriving in today's competitive market. It arms aspiring entrepreneurs with the necessary knowledge and tools to navigate the complexities of business formation. From drafting your first business plan to preparing for incorporation, this book delivers invaluable insights and practical advice to establish a strong foundation and sustain growth.

Mark Your Territory:
Navigating Trademarks in the Modern Marketplace

The second book in the Empire Builders Series: Masterclass in Business and Law is "Mark Your Territory: Navigating Trademarks in the Modern Marketplace."

Summary:

"Mark Your Territory" provides an indispensable resource for anyone involved in the branding and legal aspects of their business, offering a comprehensive guide to understanding, acquiring, and effectively managing trademarks. This book is crucial for ensuring that trademarks, which are vital assets to any business, are properly protected and leveraged.

Part 1: Fundamentals of Trademarks – Introduces the basics of trademarks, including their legal framework, the process of trademark selection and registration, and their importance in identifying business sources and ensuring product quality.

Part 2: Strategic Trademark Management – Focuses on the ongoing management of trademarks, detailing strategies for maintaining rights, monitoring for infringements, addressing challenges in digital marketing, and managing global trademark portfolios.

Part 3: Advanced Topics in Trademarks – Delves into more complex issues such as preventing trademark dilution, managing renewals, understanding the specific needs of service marks in advertising, and navigating the intricacies of trademark licensing and emerging legal trends.

Part 4: Practical Tools and Resources – Provides practical aids like sample trademark filings, management checklists, and insightful case studies, equipping readers with tangible tools and real-world examples to apply the concepts discussed effectively.

Designed for entrepreneurs, business owners, and legal professionals, "Mark Your Territory" equips readers with actionable strategies and essential tools for effective trademark management. It ensures that readers can maintain their brand's uniqueness and legal protections, thus securing a competitive edge in the marketplace.

From Idea to Empire: Mastering the Art of Business Planning

The third book in the Empire Builders Series: Masterclass in Business and Law is "From Idea to Empire: Mastering the Art of Business Planning."

Summary:

"From Idea to Empire" offers an indispensable roadmap for entrepreneurs eager to transform their innovative ideas into successful businesses. This comprehensive guide equips readers with a strategic blueprint for drafting robust business plans that attract investors and serve as a roadmap for navigating the transition from startup to thriving enterprise.

Part 1: Conceptualizing Your Business – This section lays the groundwork by assisting readers in defining their business vision, understanding market needs, analyzing competitors, and setting clear business objectives. It also guides readers in selecting an effective business model that aligns with their long-term goals.

Part 2: Strategic Planning – Delve into creating detailed marketing strategies, operational plans, and financial projections. This part covers risk management and technological integration, ensuring the business plan is both innovative and executable.

Part 3: Articulating Your Plan – Focuses on the actual drafting of the business plan, including how to write an engaging executive summary, develop compelling proposals, and master communication and negotiation tactics with potential investors and partners.

Part 4: Execution and Review – Outlines the necessary steps to launch the business successfully, monitor its performance, and make adjustments based on real-world feedback and market dynamics. This section also explores strategies for sustainable growth and long-term viability.

"From Idea to Empire" is more than a mere planning manual; it's a strategic guide that provides budding entrepreneurs with the necessary knowledge, tools, and confidence to build a business capable of facing today's market complexities. With practical advice, real-world examples, and essential resources, this book is a vital tool for anyone ready to evolve their business concept from idea to a profitable empire.

Beyond the Pen: Copyright Strategies for Modern Creators

The fourth book in the Empire Builders Series: Masterclass in Business and Law is "Beyond the Pen: Copyright Strategies for Modern Creators."

Summary:

"Beyond the Pen" serves as a crucial guide for artists, writers, musicians, and digital creators who seek to effectively navigate the complexities of copyright law and protect their creative assets. This comprehensive resource provides a deep dive into the mechanisms, legal frameworks, and strategic practices necessary to safeguard intellectual property in today's rapidly evolving digital landscape.

Part 1: Understanding Copyright Law – This section lays the groundwork by covering the essentials of copyright, including how to register works, the extent of legal protection available, and the nuances of international copyright laws. It equips creators with the crucial knowledge needed to assert and defend their rights.

Part 2: Navigating Use and Fair Use – Focuses on the vital concept of fair use, offering real-world scenarios and detailed guidance on how to handle copyright infringements and resolve disputes effectively without compromising creative freedom.

Part 3: Licensing and Monetization – Explores strategic approaches to structuring and managing licensing agreements, understanding diverse revenue models, and handling collaborations, ensuring creators can monetize their works effectively while maintaining control over their usage.

Part 4: Copyright in the Digital Age – Addresses the challenges and opportunities presented by new technologies, digital rights management, and online content sharing platforms. This part also examines the impact of social media on copyright and anticipates future trends that could influence creators' rights.

"Beyond the Pen" is more than just a legal manual; it is a strategic resource that empowers creators to protect, manage, and prosper with their intellectual property in today's interconnected market. Packed with practical examples, expert advice, and actionable strategies, this book is an indispensable tool for anyone looking to navigate the legal challenges and seize the opportunities in the modern creative landscape.

Legal Ink: Navigating the Legalese of Publishing

The fifth book in the Empire Builders Series: Masterclass in Business and Law is "Legal Ink: Navigating the Legalese of Publishing."

Summary:

"Legal Ink" offers an indispensable guide for authors seeking to navigate the complex world of publishing contracts. This comprehensive book demystifies legal jargon and provides a clear roadmap to understanding and managing the intricacies of publishing agreements effectively.

Part 1: The Grant of Rights – This section explains the various types of publishing rights, offering guidance on how to negotiate and manage these rights effectively to safeguard the author's interests.

Part 2: Your Obligations – Details the commitments authors must uphold under publishing contracts. It emphasizes the implications of these obligations for an author's literary career and advises on managing multiple contractual commitments.

Part 3: Getting Your Book to Market – Covers the practical aspects of the publishing process from the final manuscript preparation to marketing and distribution. This part ensures authors understand the steps involved and their roles in bringing their book to market.

Part 4: Follow the Money – Breaks down the financial components of publishing contracts, including advances, royalties, and accounting clauses. It offers crucial advice on how to negotiate for fair compensation.

Part 5: Parting Ways – Discusses strategies for effectively managing the conclusion of a publishing agreement, including rights reversion and contract termination, providing tactics for authors to regain control of their work.

"Legal Ink" acts as more than just a guide—it's a strategic tool for any author looking to deeply understand and master the legal framework of publishing contracts. With this book, writers are equipped to make informed decisions, negotiate better terms, and ensure their rights are protected throughout their publishing journey. It is an essential resource for anyone looking to confidently handle the legalities of publishing and secure the success of their work in the competitive marketplace.

LORI ANN MOESZINGER also known as simply "L" is the face behind the AuthorsDoor: *Publisher & Her World* books and courses. The courses are on the same topics that her books cover; and so, Secrets, Websites, Blog Sites, Social Media, Multimedia, Metadata, and Publishing. Her advanced books and courses teach Writing, Marketing, Advertising, Branding, and Publicity. Her courses are *free*; books and course workbooks are available for purchase. She has been launching the careers of self-publishers since 2009, and she also writes the AuthorsRedDoor.com blog on writing, publishing, and marketing. L is also the co-founder of The Ridge Publishing Group and its imprints.

She is an American author, publisher, and creator who resides in Coeur d'Alene, Idaho, with her husband and two dogs. She writes under the pseudonyms: Ann Patterson for her business law pieces; L. A. Moeszinger for her writing, publishing, and marketing pieces; Lori Ann Moeszinger for her biblical books and personal pieces; and a handful of others for her Manhattan Diaries series. She believes strongly in faith, blessings, and working her butt off . . . and she thinks one of the best things about being an author-publisher—unlike the lawyer she used to be—is that she can let her passion out.

Original Package Design
© 2024 AuthorsDoor Leadership Program
Cover Design: Eric Moeszinger
Author Photo © 2023 Edwin Wolfe

Parent Website: https://www.RidgePublishingGroup.com and

blog site https://www.PublisherAndHerWorld.com

Publisher Website: https://www.GuardiansofBiblicalTruth.com and

blog site https://www.Jesus-Says.com

Author website: https://www.LAMoeszinger.com and New Youniversity sites:

https://www.NewYouniversity.com, https://www.ManhattanChronicles.com

Bridge Website: https://www.AuthorsDoor.com and

blog site https://www.AuthorsRedDoor.com

Entertainment website: https://www.EthanFoxBooks.com and

blog site https://www.KidsStagram.com

This

book was art

directed by John Jared.

The art for both the cover and the

interior was created using pastels on toned

print making paper. The text was set in 10 point Times

New Roman, a typeface based on the sixteenth-century type designs

of Claude Garamond, redrawn by Robert Slimback in 1989.

The book was printed at Amazon and IngramSpark.

The Managing Editor was Jack Clark. The

Production was supervised by

Jason Reed and Ed

Warren.

www.ingramcontent.com/pod-product-compliance
Lightning Source LLC
Chambersburg PA
CBHW032055020426
42335CB00011B/350